Twin Connections

Twin Connections

✦

Stories that Celebrate the Mysterious
Bond Between Twins

Debbie LaChusa

Foreword by Susan M. Heim

iUniverse, Inc.
New York Lincoln Shanghai

Twin Connections
Stories that Celebrate the Mysterious Bond Between Twins

iUniverse books may be ordered through booksellers or by contacting:

iUniverse
2021 Pine Lake Road, Suite 100
Lincoln, NE 68512
www.iuniverse.com
1-800-Authors (1-800-288-4677)

Because of the dynamic nature of the Internet, any Web addresses or links contained in this book may have changed since publication and may no longer be valid.

The views expressed in this work are solely those of the author and do not necessarily reflect the views of the publisher, and the publisher hereby disclaims any responsibility for them.

ISBN: 978-0-595-47944-3

Printed in the United States of America

To all the twins and parents of twins who opened their hearts and lives to share their stories for this book, and to my twin sister Valerie, without whom this book would not exist.

Contents

Foreword

Susan M. Heim

When I was pregnant with my twin sons, Austen and Caleb, I wondered if they would have that special bond that some twins seem to have—that emotional connection that goes beyond most sibling relationships. Because my twins are fraternal, I had my doubts that they would share this bond. After all, I was told, they would be just like any other siblings except they happened to share a womb and a birthday. They don't share the same DNA, as identical twins do. And, indeed, I found after they were born that they are very different, not only in appearance, but in personality.

For the first few years of their lives, there was still no evidence of a twin bond. In fact, when they were babies, they almost seemed oblivious to each other's existence! But now that they are preschoolers, I'm beginning to see amazing signs of a "twin connection"! For instance, Caleb wasn't sleeping well when his bed was on one side of the room and his brother's bed was on the other side. Five nights in a row, we found Caleb sleeping with his brother in his little toddler bed, the two of them entwined together. So we moved their beds side-by-side. Amazingly, they both went right to sleep in their own beds and slept beautifully! Apparently, they just needed to be closer together.

One day, I kept Caleb home from preschool because he had a cold. At first, he was fine and seemed to enjoy his "alone time" with me, but after a few hours he started saying, "I want my Austen. I want my Austen!" It was obvious he was feeling lonely without his twin around, and he was overjoyed when they were together again!

Both boys now chatter up a storm, but Austen doesn't speak as clearly as his brother. When Austen says something we just can't understand, we often turn to Caleb and ask him to "translate." Even though Caleb speaks much more clearly than Austen, he can understand his brother every time!

As I was collecting stories and doing research for my books, *It's Twins! Parent-to-Parent Advice from Infancy Through Adolescence* and *Twice the Love: Stories of Inspiration for Families with Twins, Multiples, and Singletons*, I came across a large number of stories demonstrating this special bond between twins. Although researchers have yet to uncover any scientific evidence of any sort of psychic connection between multiples, families with twins nearly always feel differently, and have the anecdotal evidence to prove it! How can one explain the pain that a twin feels when his co-twin breaks his arm … in another state? Or the number of times that twins show up in identical shirts when they never consulted each other as to their wardrobe selections? These amazing stories are all the "proof" many people need to show that twins do, indeed, have a very special bond.

So, when I learned that Debbie LaChusa—a fraternal twin herself—was collecting stories about the amazing "twin connection," I felt compelled to read them to see if they really illustrated that wonderful bond. When I read that one woman felt her sister's pregnancy contractions and another twin knew the moment his twin had passed away although he was nowhere near him, I was convinced. Fraternal or identical, it matters not. Twins share a relationship that will always carry them through life with a friend by their side, someone who knows them like no other. I know that gives me comfort when I think of my own twins advancing through the difficult teen years and on into adulthood.

Whether you're a twin yourself, or a friend or relative of twins, I'm certain you'll enjoy these true and incredible tales of "twin connections"!

Susan M. Heim is the author of *It's Twins! Parent-to-Parent Advice from Infancy Through Adolescence* and *Twice the Love: Stories of Inspiration for Families with Twins, Multiples and Singletons.* She writes an online column for Mommies Magazine called "Loving and Living with Twins and Multiples." She is an expert on parenting twins and multiples for AllExperts.com. Susan has established a website at www.TwinsTalk.com where parents of multiples can share advice, stories and tips for raising twins, triplets and more. She is now collecting stories for *Chicken Soup for the Soul of Twins!* Please visit www.susanheim.com.

Acknowledgment

I would like to thank Susan Heim for her generous help compiling and editing all of my twin stories and facts into a truly wonderful book.

Introduction

Whether it's the way they finish each other's sentences, know when their twin is in trouble, feel the other's pain, or seem to have uncanny parallels in their lives, there is definitely a connection between twins unlike any other sibling relationship I've seen or experienced.

My name is Debbie LaChusa, and I'm a fraternal twin. My twin sister, Valerie, and I are now in our forties, so we've had many years to share our wonderful twin connection. I've never been able to explain the bond we share or the parallels in our lives.

I always wanted to know if other twins experienced the same things that we did. After all, we had this connection—and we weren't even that close at times—so I wondered about the bond between other twins, especially those who were identical.

This curiosity led me to develop the Twin Connections website and to begin collecting stories from twins around the world. I wanted to know more about this twin connection that Valerie and I shared, and to see if other twins had the same experiences. I had heard rumors and stories about twins feeling each other's pain and reading each other's minds, and I wanted to find out if they were more than just rumors.

As the stories started pouring into my website, I began to realize they weren't just rumors. I have been contacted by twins and parents of twins from all around the world. Some shared their amazing stories and unexplainable connections; others shared their sadness and heartache because they've lost their twin. Parents shared stories of the amazing connections they have witnessed between their infant twins. And the one commonality among all of the stories was that unique connection that twins share. While it cannot be explained, it is very real.

These stories have helped me to understand that there is something special about twins. Whether the connection they share is genetic, the result of spending nine months together in the womb, or due to being raised together as siblings of the same age or same gender, I don't know. And, for me, the reason is not important. It's less about understanding the twin connection, and more about verifying its existence and celebrating it.

The stories I've received definitely confirm that the "twin connection" exists. These tales have also made me laugh, cry and feel proud to be a member of this very special club.

Sprinkled throughout this book, you will also find the results of a survey I conducted among 100 twins who are members of my Twin Connections website. They comment on issues such as whether they dress alike, how close they are to their twin, whether they have a strong bond, and what they like and dislike about being twins. I found the results of the survey enlightening, and I think you'll agree that these fun facts help shed more light on the mysterious twin connection.

In this book, you will read story after story from twins young and old, fraternal and identical, living and dead. I guarantee some will amaze you. Some will baffle you. Some will make you cry. And others will simply bring a smile to your face.

But first I'd like to take a moment to share my own story. I hope it helps you understand why I felt compelled to learn more about the "twin connection."

My Twin Story

My parents say I used to copy everything my "older" twin sister Valerie did (she is five minutes older than I am) when I was a baby. Here's what else my mom, Joan McKasson, had to say about raising my sister and me:

My husband, Dale, and I had the girls on November eleventh, less than one year after we were married on December 26, 1960. We wanted to start our family right away, so you can imagine our delight when we discovered that I was pregnant with twins. Twins were not as common in the sixties as they are now. The grandparents-to-be were very excited as well. When it came time to bring the girls home from the hospital after they were born, I asked Dale to bring the beautiful baby comforters that we had been given. I didn't think about how slippery the comforters were. I remember sitting in a wheelchair, a beautiful baby girl in each arm, ready to go home and praying that they would not slide out of their covers.

Once home, we had many bottles of formula to prepare and lots of diapers to wash and fold. There were no pre-folded diapers in those days, and we did not have diaper service. I always remember when Dale made a double batch of formula late at night, and left it on the stove to cool as directed so he could put it in the refrigerator. He fell asleep and had to pour all the formula down the kitchen drain because we were afraid it had spoiled. He started over at 2:00 AM and made a new batch. That was a labor of love from a brand-new father.

Keeping these two babies on some kind of feeding schedule so that Mom and Dad could get a chance to eat dinner became a challenge, but Dad came up with an idea! He tied a string to the mobile over Debbie's bed, ran the string through the living room, and attached it to the kitchen table. Because Debbie was the smaller of the twins, she would wake up first, fuss, cry, and wake Valerie who was still sleeping soundly. When Debbie started to fuss, all Dad had to do was tug the string, and the mobile would move. Debbie would be distracted, and Valerie got a little more sleep before she woke up. Meanwhile, Mom and Dad got a few bites of dinner before it got too cold.

When the girls were just old enough to walk and get into trouble, they were playing in their bedroom one day. All of a sudden, it became way too quiet. I walked in to see that Valerie and Debbie were having great fun pulling all my nicely folded diapers from the shelves where I had neatly stacked them. Of course, I had to refold all those diapers and stack them up again. I can still see that funny picture in my mind!

As any twin and all mothers of twins know, Debbie and Valerie were great companions and always had someone to play with. Of course, there were fights—hair pulling and sibling rivalry—but they also had a lot of fun. They have given us many good memories.

◆   ◆   ◆

Our parents did a great job of raising my sister and me with our own sense of identity and did not dress us alike. We developed unique personalities, and had our own interests and friends.

As Teens, Our Relationship Was Strained

In junior high and high school, we drifted apart. We had our own friends and didn't even hang out together in school. Valerie seemed to rebel a bit against having a twin. And, for the most part, most people at school didn't even know we were sisters. Ironically, many people thought my best friend at the time was my sister! And when they found out Valerie was my sister—and was actually my twin—they were shocked! As fraternal twins, we didn't look that much alike.

Looking back, I can now see that being teen twins put us into a very competitive relationship. We competed for grades, friends, attention, boys—you name it. We shared a bedroom, and overall it was a tough time for the two of us. We were still friends, and we did do things together, but our relationship was definitely strained during our teen years. I often wonder if the same thing would have happened if we had been identical twins.

Our Connection Returned When We Became Adults

Both my sister and I moved out of our parents' home at relatively young ages. Valerie moved out at age eighteen, and I married and moved out at age nineteen. The interesting thing is that once we both moved out on our own, we became close again, and that's when our connection really began showing up.

There would be days I would be thinking of calling Valerie, and seconds later the phone would ring, and it would be her on the other end. It happened so often back then that we often joked about it. For us, being separated seemed to make our connection stronger.

When We Got Married, Other Interesting Connections Began to Appear

A rather odd connection we share has to do with our married last names. We both married men with "capital letter in the middle" last names. For me, it was LaChusa. For my sister, it was DuBois. Now that might not seem like a big deal, but we also grew up with the "capital letter in the middle" last name of McKasson.

McKasson wasn't a bad name, but it was the kind of last name that always seemed to complicate matters. People either didn't capitalize the "K," or they split our last name into two words. I felt as though I was forever correcting people. How I longed for a simple last name like Smith!

We figured when we got married we would finally get "regular" last names. Well, guess what? It didn't happen! We both got new "capital letter in the middle" last names! My sister did later remarry and now she has a "regular" last name, but our connection doesn't end there.

Now We Aren't the Only Ones Who Share a Birthday

Our connection has manifested itself in an interesting way through our husbands, in addition to the whole last name thing.

Our husbands also share the same birthday (no, they're not twins!), they are both left-handed, they both wear glasses, and they both graduated from the same high school. Pretty weird, huh?!

Our children share some similarities as well. We both have outgoing, athletic daughters. And our sons tend to be more reserved, shy, and are probably the most finicky eaters you could ever find. We often commiserate about the challenge of feeding them and joke that the two of them could live on a diet of chicken fingers and pizza!

We've Had Our Challenges, Too

Growing up, there were definitely times I wished I wasn't a twin, when I didn't want to share the attention, especially at birthdays, graduations and other special occasions. It was tough always having to share the spotlight. In fact, I remember one thing I really enjoyed about my wedding (and actually, I didn't even realize it until after the fact) was that it was the first time I didn't have to share the spotlight with my sister. The spotlight was on me, and just me. Before that, it was always "Debbie and Valerie." My twin sister was still in my wedding party, of course, but it wasn't equal billing.

Like any friendship or sibling relationship, we've had our ups and downs. But I wouldn't trade my twin sister and our wonderful connection for anything in the world. I am lucky to live near her and her family, and to have her in my life.

One thing that all of the stories in this book have made me realize is that every set of twins has their own unique connection. It is not better or stronger than other twins; it is just different. And every twin should cherish, appreciate, and celebrate this wonderful "twin connection."

Shared Sickness, Pain ... and Pregnancy!

A twin hits his head, and his sister gets an excruciating headache. A woman goes into labor, and her twin sister shares her pain! A twin needs a life-saving transplant, and guess who's a perfect match? Health-care crises aren't solo events when it comes to twins!

The Power of Two
Anabel Stenzel

My identical twin sister, Isabel, and I were born with a genetic disorder called cystic fibrosis (CF), one of the most common life-threatening genetic disorders affecting more than 35,000 Americans. A genetic defect in cells results in thick mucus that clogs the lungs and digestive tract. Symptoms include frequent pneumonia and breathing difficulties, poor absorption of nutrients and intestinal obstructions. We were diagnosed at birth because I was born with a bowel obstruction, which is a classic sign of CF. Since childhood, we have been hospitalized frequently for intravenous antibiotics and had to do breathing treatments four times a day. These treatments consisted of inhaling medications to open the lungs and thin the mucus. We also did physical therapy on our chests, in which our parents had to pat our backs to help loosen the thick mucus so we could cough it out. By our mid-twenties, we had been hospitalized more than thirty times for pneumonia. Despite aggressive care, we were plagued with congestion and coughing fits. We were often hospitalized together so we kept each other company. As twins, we shared the disease; we helped each other with treatments and motivated each other to stay disciplined with our health care. It was a true blessing to be twins.

Even though we had the same medical regimen and disease, my disease progressed more rapidly, and by my mid-twenties I had a lung capacity of less than 30 percent due to progressive lung disease. I began requiring oxygen to walk and sleep. Simple tasks, such as walking or grocery shopping, became difficult due to shortness of breath. After an extensive evaluation, I was placed on a lung transplant wait-list at Stanford Hospital. On June 14, 2000, after sixteen months of being actively listed, I received the gift that changed my life forever.

My donor was a twenty-nine-year-old man who passed away from a brain aneurysm. His family made the selfless act of organ donation at a time of personal tragedy. My surgery was performed by Dr. Bruce Reitz and took more than nine hours. Fortunately, there were no immediate surgical complications, and I left the hospital within two weeks. Immediate challenges included adjusting to the side effects of the anti-rejection medications and trying to inflate my new lungs.

Since my recovery period, the gift of transplantation has been manifested daily. By five months post-transplant, I was able to return to work as a genetic counselor at Stanford Hospital. Since then, I have bought a home and fallen in love. I discovered the joy of backpacking and have hiked in the Sierra Nevada Mountains in California. I joined a swim team and learned to jog. Exploring the world became another passion, and I have visited six foreign countries and seventeen states with my new lungs.

While I enjoyed good health for the first time, I was witnessing my sister's disease progress as well. She began to have complications of CF, like lung bleeds, which occur when the lung infections invade the pulmonary blood vessels. She required oxygen and was unable to walk long distances. In early 2004, Isabel was hospitalized for pneumonia. Despite five intravenous antibiotics, her condition deteriorated rapidly, and she was put on a waiting list for a lung transplant. However, a week later, Isabel suffered a sudden respiratory arrest. I was in the room at the time, and witnessed her crossing over and shouting for loved ones who had previously passed away. It was an intense and emotional experience to witness my own twin dying. Luckily, she was saved after being put on a ventilator, a machine that breathed for her. She remained on the ventilator for seven days while we waited for a donor lung to be available. After seven days, she would be deemed too sick to survive the surgery. At the eleventh hour, a donor lung became available, and Isabel received the gift of life. It was the happiest day of my life when my sister woke up in the Intensive Care Unit and asked, "Did I just have a transplant?"

Lung transplants are one of the most complex and risky of all solid organ transplants. Survival rates are approximately 50 percent in five years. We both vigilantly take our anti-rejection medications daily, exercise every day, and eat healthy diets. Because we are immuno-suppressed to avoid rejecting our donor lungs, we are careful to avoid sick people and wash our hands frequently to minimize the risk of infections.

Together, Isabel and I are living normal lives for the first time ever. We have climbed Half Dome in Yosemite together and have written a memoir about our experiences entitled *The Power of Two: A Twin Triumph over Cystic Fibrosis,* which was published in November 2007. We have no more medical treatments, pneumonia, intravenous antibiotics or coughing. Life is like a dream, and we are so privileged to be alive. As far back as I can remember, every time my twin and I celebrated a birthday together, we would blow out our birthday candles with the same wish for health. The lifelong wish we had not to cough or be short of breath has come true.

For more information, see www.stenzeltwins.com.

◆   ◆   ◆

Sisters Share Bloody Nose

Jenni Montoya
Farmington, Minnesota

My four-year-old twin daughter, Lexie, fell off her scooter yesterday and bumped her face on the sidewalk. Her left nostril was bleeding. As she and I sat on the front step while I held a tissue to her nose, my other twin, Bella, stepped in front of us and said, "Mom, I have a bloody nose!" I looked up, and her left nostril was bleeding, too! I'm still in awe.

◆   ◆   ◆

Twin's Hand Slammed in Door, but Her Sister Gets the Bruises!

Carol Willette Bachofner
Rockland, Maine

My twin daughters are identical, mirror-image twins. They have always had "bodily connections." *It's all a feeling,* I used to think—until my husband slammed the eldest twin's poor fingers in the car door. She, of course, yelped right away, and he felt terrible. Her sister yelped, too. We were used to that. What we were NOT expecting was that the younger twin would get a crease across her fingers! That's right: twin A got slammed, and twin B got the crease and the bruises! We have been scratching our heads over that one for years! Oh, and since they are mirror-image twins, the twin who got the crease and bruises got them on the OPPOSITE hand! Go figure!

Surgery in Synch
Brittani Evans
East Newark, New Jersey

My twin sister and I have always been close. We are twenty years old. I am four minutes older than her. When my mother was pregnant, the doctors did not know that she was having twins. She was huge, but when they ran the tests, my sister was sharing my mother's heartbeat and they didn't even know she was there.

It was a huge surprise when I was born and the doctor saw another leg. Ever since then, we have been extremely close. For a long time, we could not even sleep if we were not together. Although we had two cribs, we would only sleep if we were sleeping together. We also shared a full-size bed until we were about thirteen years old.

We have gone through everything together and have had many instances of "twin connections." We have had the same nightmares and dreams, completed each other's sentences, and known when something was wrong with each other.

The most eerie situation happened in June 2006. I had surgery on my ankle the day before our twentieth birthday. My surgery was scheduled for the morning, and my sister had to work in the afternoon. I told her she did not have to go to the hospital with me, that I would be fine. So she told me she would see me when she got home from work that night.

I left for the hospital where they gave me a Valium to calm me down enough to insert an IV. (I am a big baby.) They placed me on a bed and administered the IV in my left hand. Around that time, my twin was out shopping for my "Get Well" stuff with my younger sister and kept complaining that her left hand was killing her. She even had our younger sister look at it for a bruise, but there was none.

Later on, before she went to work, she met my parents and a few of our friends at a diner near the hospital for brunch while I was in surgery. Right before they took me into the operating room, they asked me to sign a release form to have a nerve block put in. I agreed and signed it. The nerve block numbs your entire leg so that you have no pain for about twenty hours after surgery. No one knew that I was going to get the nerve block. At lunch, my sister turned to a close friend of the family and complained that she could not feel her leg at all. Both of these things could be easily explained if she were at the hospital or with me up until the point that I went in the operating room, but she wasn't. She had no idea which hand the IV was in, and she had never even heard of a nerve block before I told her about it when I woke up.

There are plenty of instances like these in our lives, so much so that we freak out most people when we start to tell them! Some friends of our family, who are parents of toddler twins, often ask us to explain things that their babies are doing, and we can.

I love being a twin, although sometimes it is very trying. We are so close that we often get under each other's skin, but the next day we are back to doing just about everything together.

◆   ◆   ◆

I Like Being a Twin Because ...

The bond is so strong, and I know I'm never alone.

◆   ◆   ◆

Pain of Broken Arm Hits Twins
Jill Vaught
Crane, Indiana

Our names are Jack and Jill, like the storybook, and we were each other's best friends growing up. When we became teenagers, we drifted our own ways. Jack went into the service, and I got married. I moved to Okinawa, Japan, for three years, and when I came home, Jack moved a two-and-a-half-hour drive away from me. However, we just couldn't seem to get the old bond back.

Then one day I took my boys fishing. I had an extraordinary pain shoot through my left arm. Three places in my arm hurt very badly. I couldn't figure it out as I had done nothing to the arm to make it hurt so. As quickly as the pain came, it left, and I forgot about it and just wrote it off as a fluke.

A couple of days later, I was talking with my mother on the phone, and she told me that Jack had fallen off some scaffolding at work and had been injured. Without missing a beat, I said, "He broke his left arm in three places, didn't he?" I was right. I told my mother of the incident with my arm a couple of days before, and she said we always did have a special connection!

◆   ◆   ◆

I *Don't* Like Being a Twin Because …

We feel each other's pain. It's like living two lives instead of one.

◆   ◆   ◆

Twins Battle Rare Marfan Syndrome
Rod Pollard
Dryden, Ontario, Canada

My twin brother and I were born with a very rare condition called Marfan Syndrome. I do believe we are the only twins with this condition.

We were told that we would probably not survive the first few years of life, but being so stubborn, we surpassed that. Then we were told we would not live past age twenty because of the serious effects from the syndrome, but needless to say, we are still sticking it out at age thirty-five.

Up until a few years ago, our conditions grew worse and worse. There is no known cure or treatment for this syndrome, and we were told that we would need immediate heart surgery, or we would die from this condition. So, in November 2003, we were the first twins to have our aortic roots replaced with synthetic ones.

My twin brother was the second person and I was the third to have this procedure done in Canada. You can imagine the surprise of the surgeon to have twins undergo such a procedure at the same time! Even though we were given extremely low odds of surviving the surgeries, we beat the odds again and survived. We are still currently undergoing complications from the surgery, but we are coping.

Even though we still face many obstacles from this syndrome, we will continue to fight the battle. Along with problems from the syndrome, we are coping with other injuries and conditions from normal day-to-day wear and tear, and it is to the point that doctors and specialists won't treat us. My twin brother has been waiting to have a stomach hernia repair for over three years. Normal people can get this procedure done in about six weeks, but because of our high-risk condition, no surgeon wants to perform the surgery. But the hernia won't go away by itself, and is on the verge of bursting.

We both worked the same type of job in the auto reconditioning field for over eleven years until our injuries got the better of us. We are now both on disability pensions.

We have always lived with each other, and we both drive modified station wagons—that is, until recently, when my twin brother's doctor pulled his license because of little mini strokes that they won't confirm or treat him for. Again, we can't find a neurologist who can diagnose and treat my brother.

It is a four-hour trip, East and West of us, to see specialists, and most of the time, our trips are wasted because of misdiagnoses. It is quite hard for me to drive all the time to get to these appointments. I have kept a journal of a lot of these situations, and when I read through them again, I just have to laugh. If any publisher is interested in writing a book or a movie about twins and their hardships, look me up. I've got a lot of good tales to tell!

When you smile at the world, the world smiles back at you ... well, in our case, most of the time.

To learn more about Marfan Syndrome, visit www.marfan.org.

◆   ◆   ◆

I Like Being a Twin Because ...

We have been through some hard times that I believe would have driven us apart permanently without the "twin bond."

◆   ◆   ◆

Love for a Handicapped Sister
Linda Real
Sun Valley, Idaho

My twin sister is mentally handicapped. We are fifty years old. She has lived in group homes and institutions for the last thirty-five years. Now that my mother is old, I moved my dear sister out of the state she had always been in to live near me. My husband and I work full-time and have children, so we were unable to take her full-time since she requires twenty-four-hour care.

I love my sister dearly, and she is somewhat of a savant in music. We spend as much time together now as we can. She is also a diabetic, and I had to learn how to give her insulin shots. Being that I hate needles, I overcame this fear for the love of my sister.

My twin and I have a deep connection, and I will care for her and love her for the rest of my life. Two years ago, she almost died and was on life support for four months, which tore my heart out. My twin responded to me by waking up from her coma, and I knew I had to help her fight for her life. Today, she sits at the piano again and plays so well. I am happy to have my twin back!

◆   ◆   ◆

Twin Feels When Brother Takes a Beating
Kelly
Staten Island, New York

My twin brother and I always went to school together from the time we were little. But when we began high school, we ended up going to different schools. One day as I was leaving school, I started to get terrible pains in my nose, the back of my head, around my eyes, and in my ribs.

On my way home, I received a phone call to get to the hospital as soon as I could because my brother had been beat up in school, and the boys did very severe damage. When I arrived at the hospital, they informed me that my brother had a shattered nose, broken eye sockets and cheekbones, a fractured skull, and possibly cracked ribs. I couldn't believe what I was hearing.

I had felt pain in all the same places that my brother did.

◆   ◆   ◆

I Like Being a Twin Because ...

I have someone who has been with me forever and always will be close to me, no matter what happens.

◆   ◆   ◆

A Double Hangover!
Kimberly
Jamestown, New York

My twin and I were born two months and eight days before our due date. Allison was born fourteen minutes before me. Our mom didn't know she was having twins until four or five weeks before we were born, so you could say that I was a surprise.

Anyway, our mom would tell us stories of how when we were younger, we could read each other's minds and feel each other's pain. When Alli had to get stitches and they put the numbing stuff on her head, I was at home and I started to scream because I could feel it.

Nevertheless, I didn't really believe our mom until recently. One weekend, our mom went out of town with our younger sister, and our dad was working. We decided to have a bonfire with some people we know from high school and work. Well, my twin sister had a lot to drink while I just sat there and drank Pepsi because I never liked drinking. The next day, I woke up, had a horrible headache and felt really sick, and my sister didn't feel a thing. I got her hangover!

We are children number 4 and 5 out of six kids, and we are really close. We shared a room our whole lives until our family got a new house, and then we got different rooms. One night we were sleeping in the backyard in a tent with our younger sister, and I didn't want to sleep out there anymore so I went in the house. The next day, I woke up and my twin was in the house, too.

We do share almost everything, but there are things we don't agree on. I think it would be cool to marry a twin and she doesn't, but that's okay. I think it is cool that we have a close bond, and we have each other to confide in when we have problems.

◆   ◆   ◆

Twin Survey: How strong is your connection with your twin?

We do not have a connection at all	4.2%
We occasionally have a connection	36.5%
We feel each other's pain	40.6%
We know what the other is thinking	53.1%
We sense when the other is in trouble	57.3%

NOTE: Combined percentages are greater than 100 because respondents were allowed to select more than one answer.

◆   ◆   ◆

Twin and His Dog Feel Brother's Anxiety
Artie Miller
Hanover Park, Illinois

My brother and I are forty-seven-year-old twins. I now live in Chicago; he still lives on Long Island. We are both married and work in related fields. We have always had a connection, being close and able to know when the other is having trouble. You know, that "twin thing" ... Whenever either one of us has one of those moments when anxiety strikes, the other one knows that something generally is going on, and soon after there is a call. It is creepy at times.

I try to stay pretty mellow; my brother is a bit higher strung. I have three dachshunds: a mom, dad and puppy. The mom, Miss Tea, a six-year-old dachshund, has a seizure whenever anxiety strikes me and I am near her. She gets all tense, her muscles tighten, and she loses bladder control. It's really bad until we can calm her down, which my wife and daughters are good at doing. When this happens, I feel really guilty, which doesn't help her!

More and more often, when my brother has an anxiety attack, I feel an unexplained tenseness for no apparent reason, and my dog has a seizure. For example, in the summer, my family likes to camp. I was changing the locks on our trailer bins, and I was on the last of seven. The sun was shining, the sky was blue, and it was a wonderfully cool early summer morning in the Midwest. My wife and kids were still in their PJs in the trailer when I felt tenseness come over me and thoughts of my brother. I could not explain it since I was almost done with such a simple task.

Minutes later, my daughter stuck her head out and said that Miss Tea was having a seizure. We calmed her down, and I called my brother in New York. He had a ton of kids over playing with his son, with a driveway full of bikes, scooters and whatnot. His wife was coming home with loads of groceries, and he was behind on all kinds of things to do. He was not having a great start to his day. I asked him to calm down since he was driving my dog crazy!

Last evening, in the kitchen, Miss Tea leaned over on her side against the cabinet. She was all tight and having a seizure. I was tense, attempting to stay calm, but not really knowing why I was tense in the first place. We calmed her down, and then I called my brother, who was running late. His family was waiting. There was lots of traffic, and he was trying to figure out what they would be doing for dinner before karate practice. I again asked him to stay calm and offered to call our veterinarian to give him something to stay calm!

◆   ◆   ◆

I *Don't* Like Being a Twin Because ...

My twin knows how to push my buttons better than anyone else.

◆   ◆   ◆

One Is Pregnant, but the Other Has the Symptoms!
Angelina
Fort Saskatchewan, Alberta, Canada

When I became pregnant with my first son, I was living a couple of hours away from my family. I seemed to have a perfect pregnancy with no morning sickness, infections (kidney, bladder, etc.), or pains at all. Unfortunately, my twin sister was not as fortunate as she experienced everything—even though she was not pregnant! She even experienced false labor for me. Throughout my pregnancy, she was the one who looked and felt pregnant, except that I had the big belly. She even went for numerous pregnancy tests to prove she was not pregnant!

◆   ◆   ◆

Twin Seeks Sister After Surgery
Karen Walsh
Wakefield, Massachusetts

At twenty-six months old, one of my twins had to have surgery. It was an outpatient procedure that required her to be put under with anesthesia. After the surgery, the doctor came to the waiting room and told me she was in recovery, still groggy but I could see her.

When I entered the room, Jillian's tiny body was lifeless on the big table. She was lying on her stomach with an IV in her little hand. I went over, rubbed her back and said, "Jillian, Mommy is here. Your operation is over. I love you."

When she heard my voice, she strained to lift her head from the pillow, peeked open her eyes and said, "Bella." Then she quickly dropped her head back on the pillow and closed her eyes.

The nurse looked at me, confused and wondering who "Bella" was. I smiled and told Jillian that her twin (Isabella) was home with Daddy, and we could see them both soon.

It was at that moment that I realized, even in the subconscious state Jillian was in, that the twin connection is deeper than any bond we can imagine.

◆   ◆   ◆

Strep Throat Can't Keep Twins Apart
Katherine Dolan-Caracciola
Bayside, New York

Ryan and Nicholas, identical twin boys, were celebrating their third birthday. Each time somebody brought a gift, both boys would beg to open the presents. Because I wanted to know what gifts each person brought so I could properly send out thank-you cards, I wouldn't allow the boys to open their presents and told them we would have to leave them on the table until after the cake was cut.

As the day progressed, the presents got higher and higher as Ryan and Nicholas watched, knowing they couldn't touch them.

Finally, the cake was brought out, and the boys were told to make a wish before blowing out the candles. Can you guess what they wished for?

Without hesitation, they both said at the same time, "We wish we could open our birthday presents!"

About six months later, Ryan and Nicholas started pre-kindergarten. Neither had ever been away from the other. One day, Nicholas was sick with strep throat and a fever of 103 degrees F.

After great difficulty, I managed to talk Ryan into going to school without his brother. After I returned from dropping him off, Nicholas said, "Mommy, could you take me to school now?" I couldn't imagine why he was asking to go to school being that he was so sick.

I said, "Nicholas, you can't go to school today. You're sick!"

He replied, "I'm not as sick as much as I miss my brother!"

◆   ◆   ◆

Twin Girls Both Have "Tummy Troubles"
Rebekka Broas-Lynch
Woodbury, Minnesota

I am the mother of six-month-old twins. Last January, when my husband and I found out that I was pregnant, he joked with me about having twins, but I knew it wouldn't happen because there are no twins in our family. Plus, we got pregnant naturally. Nonetheless, I secretly hoped I would have twins.

I have a daughter from a previous marriage, but this pregnancy was very different. Subconsciously, I was very interested in twin pregnancies and would even do some research on it. Our twelve-week check-up with my OB/GYN fizzled my secret hopes when she found only one heartbeat. But something wasn't quite right.

I was a little disappointed, especially because I was already starting to show and feel movement all over, which twins would have explained. Everyone kept telling me that the second pregnancy is different, and you show faster and feel movement sooner because you know what to expect, but I wasn't convinced.

At our sixteen-week check-up, I told the doctor that I just wasn't feeling like this was a normal pregnancy, and I thought maybe they had my due date wrong.

I looked like I was already six to seven months along! But I wasn't gaining any weight, and I was exhausted all the time.

She did an external exam and measured my stomach, and again told me everything was fine and right on track. I was measuring just where I should be, and she wasn't feeling an "abnormally large baby," as she called it. So we set up an ultrasound for four weeks from then.

My husband and I had decided that we didn't want to know the sex of the baby, so when we were all ready to begin the ultrasound, I turned away from the screen and told the technician that we didn't want to know what it was. She just giggled a little and said, "You mean what THEY are!!!" I whipped my head around and saw two heads on the monitor. I think time stood still! I looked at my husband and just laughed as the tears streamed down my face. I couldn't believe that after all this time, I actually had twins. And I finally felt relief.

Everything made sense. The rest of the pregnancy went by just fine until my ultrasound at thirty-four weeks. The radiologist noticed a larger-than-normal loop of bowel on Twin A. We had to see a perinatologist for some more tests and another ultrasound. They assured us that everything was okay, and worst-case scenario was that this baby may have to be examined more thoroughly at birth.

A few more weeks went by, and I began to wonder if I would ever have the babies. My husband and I decided that we were ready and talked to our doctor about inducing labor. Since we were almost to thirty-seven weeks, and both babies were in positions to be delivered naturally, she gave us the go-ahead for an amniocentesis to see if the twins' lungs were ready.

During this procedure, the doctor noticed that the loop of bowel was quite a bit larger than it had been two weeks prior. He advised us to have a C-section right away to prevent any stress on this baby's stomach. So, at thirty-six weeks, six days, I delivered two beautiful girls, believed to be identical, although we never got official results because of the other health complications.

Kerragyn Barbara Lynch (Twin A) was five pounds, seven ounces, and Giavanna Renae Lynch (the "hidden twin" or Twin B) was five pounds, two ounces. Both were eighteen inches long and just gorgeous. I was ecstatic! The doctors examined Kerragyn and thought she looked fine. They didn't see any problems with her intestines. They sent both babies to the newborn nursery, and we were a very happy family!

Less than twenty-four hours later, Kerragyn was rushed to the NICU at Children's Hospital in St. Paul, Minnesota. Giavanna followed shortly after, both with bowel obstructions. Two days later, they were given the diagnosis of cystic fibrosis. And when Kerragyn was just five days old, she had major surgery to remove the twist in her small intestine that had developed in utero. She was left with just 68 centimeters of small intestine. (The normal baby has 200 centimeters.)

Giavanna spent four weeks in the NICU before coming home, but Kerragyn had to spend over ten weeks there. She had another surgery when she was six weeks old to repair her intestine and put a feeding tube in her stomach so we could give her extra feedings at night while she was sleeping.

The girls are doing great now, and both are almost fourteen pounds! I find it amazing how in tune they are with each other. They weren't together for the first eleven weeks of their lives, but are inseparable now! They sleep in the same crib, and don't sleep well if the other is not there. When they are playing on the floor, they reach out for each other's hand and will hold it while playing with a toy in the other!

They do everything within a day of each other. Gia started to smile and giggle, and the next morning Kerragyn laughed! When Kerragyn learned how to roll over, Giavanna did it a few hours later! Kerragyn found her voice and began to babble, and Gia started talking back! They really are my miracles!

◆   ◆   ◆

A Twin Transplant
Pamela Butler
Nashville, Tennessee

I am the mother of thirty-four-year-old twin daughters, Anna Marie and Amy Beth. Their story is unusual because we were told at their birth that they were fraternal twins.

The doctor told us there was one placenta, but the twins were in separate sacs. Anna was hospitalized for five weeks for "failure to thrive." Finally, at the third hospital she went to, they found that she only had one kidney, and that one did not work at full capacity. With medication, she quickly began to gain weight and was healthy as a child, just a little smaller than her twin sister.

People always remarked at how much they looked alike, although they were fraternal twins. By the age of eighteen, Anna was in need of a kidney transplant. The whole family was given a blood work-up, and Amy was the best match. As soon as Amy's kidney was put into Anna's body, we were told that the kidney function was as though it were put back in the same body.

Anna was given a minimum amount of anti-rejection drugs for one year, and then weaned off them. Her health has been great, and so has Amy's. Anna has given birth to two children and Amy to one, with no complications despite their having one healthy kidney each.

Miraculously, there is now no doubt that they are identical twins. We are so blessed!

◆　　　◆　　　◆

Brother's Concussion Hurts Twin Sister's Head
Jennifer Strasser
Kenmore, New York

My older brother and sister are twins. They've always had this strange bond between them. As babies, one would start crying in a room far away from the other, and the other baby would suddenly cry for no reason, too.

The most bizarre story was when the twins were in high school. My brother played soccer as the goalie for the varsity team. My sister was at home and couldn't make it to the game one night because she had to study. My brother was in a collision with another player. He suffered a concussion and had to be taken to the hospital.

Before anyone could call home to talk to my sister, she began to have a major headache and couldn't study anymore. When she got the call from the hospital, she was in bed because her head hurt so badly. It turns out that the headache started right around the time my brother got hurt at the game.

There have been several other strange occurrences throughout their lives, but that one sticks out the most in my memory.

◆　　　◆　　　◆

Labor Pains Give Twin Sister a Headache
Marcy Jervis
Rochester, Indiana

My twin story begins twenty-three years ago with the birth of my son. My twin sister was unable to have a baby because of infertility problems. I had a difficult pregnancy with gallbladder problems, three false labors, and giving birth three weeks before my due date.

My twin sister was hosting a surprise baby shower for me when I went into labor. She opened my baby gifts while I was on my way to the hospital.

The next day, I was induced, and my twin was by my side until I delivered. She could feel my pain because she experienced a migraine headache the whole time I was in labor. After the birth of my son, her headache was gone! Our son is very special to his aunt because we have shared him. He was fortunate to have two moms while growing up.

◆   ◆   ◆

I Like Being a Twin Because …

Someone knows me and loves me better than anyone else.

◆   ◆   ◆

Twins Survive Twin to Twin Transfusion Syndrome
Dale Hamilton
Grand Prairie, Texas

Last October, my daughter Lisa La Penna found out she was having twins. Her doctor scheduled her for an ultrasound at fifteen weeks. During the ultrasound, the tech found that Lisa's twins had Twin to Twin Transfusion Syndrome. Her doctor, Dr. Goldaper, told my daughter that the twins had a 10 percent chance to survive. We were devastated.

The doctor gave us several options, but the best was to go to Tampa, Florida, to see Dr Quintero. By the next Thursday, my daughter was in laser surgery with Dr Quintero. The staff at Tampa General Hospital was wonderful.

The next four months were like a roller-coaster ride, with different problems coming up during weekly ultrasounds. But finally, at thirty-five weeks, Lisa's two beautiful girls, Savannah and Morgan, were born alive and kicking. I cannot thank Dr. Quintero at Tampa General enough for saving my granddaughters' lives, and Dr. Goldaper at Medical Center of Arlington in Arlington, Texas, for directing us there.

◆   ◆   ◆

Twin Saves Sister Who Stops Breathing
Melissa
Timaru, South Canterbury, New Zealand

When my identical twin sister and I were younger, I was diagnosed with epilepsy. Before this was diagnosed, I would often experience apnea during which I'd stop breathing in my sleep.

One time when we were about two years old, I had an apnea episode. My twin sister Sonia went to our mum and saved my life by saying to her, "Mummy, Missy won't wake up!"

There are many other stories of twin-like things throughout our lives, but that one tops the list. I will never forget that my twin sister is the reason I am still here twenty years later.

◆   ◆   ◆

Twin Born with Rare Condition Begins to Thrive
Lisa Wiseman
Wyoming, Michigan

My twins, Cadia Susanne and Carmen Alberta, were born on Thanksgiving Day 2006. At thirty-four weeks, they were premature. Carmen was born with Pierre Robin Sequence (PRS), which is characterized by a combination of three features: the lower jaw is abnormally small, the tongue is displaced downward, and there is an abnormal opening in the roof of the mouth. The tongue might have a tendency to ball up in the back of the mouth, causing the airway to block and possible apnea. This happened to our daughter, and as a result, she required a tracheotomy and a feeding tube.

Cadia was born with no problems other than being premature, and she was only in the NICU for eleven days. Carmen spent sixty-eight days in the NICU and requires nursing care.

There is no known cause for PRS, and it is not something you can necessarily see on an ultrasound. Looking back, we did notice that her chin was down toward her chest, but that is not something that the ultrasound technician would usually notice.

Carmen's condition has been a bit overwhelming to say the least, especially for first-time parents. When we brought her home, there was so much to learn—cleaning her trach and feeding-tube site, changing the trach, feeding her through a tube, suctioning her trach, having her on an apnea monitor, and then having strangers in our house while we were sleeping to take care of her. And all the supplies!

She has so many doctor appointments—her regular pediatrician, her ENT doctor, cardiologist, pulmonologist, plastic surgeon, gastroenterologist, ophthalmologist, feeding therapist, physical therapist. And we want to make sure that Cadia gets enough attention, too.

Well, here we are, six-and-a-half months later, and Carmen is doing just fine. Her progress has been nothing but astounding. She is consistently gaining weight; she is off the monitor. She's moving around, rolling over and interacting with her sister. We are about six months away from having her cleft palate repaired, and then the trach and feeding tube will hopefully be removed a few months from then.

Carmen has even started to make sounds around her trach, and judging from her facial expressions, she is quite proud of herself when she does! My husband and I are now pros with her care, and we've formed relationships with our nurses. We have had such a great support system in our family and friends.

We have been blessed with two wonderful and beautiful girls, and we look forward to watching them grow and bond as sisters.

◆   ◆   ◆

Twins Have Cancer Scares at the Same Time
Jill Vaught

In November 2006, I was having real problems with my female parts. I had an ultrasound that revealed a large tumor on my left ovary. The doctors started to do tests that would show if it was cancer or not. The day I went in for the blood work, I was very shaky and unsure.

Later that night while talking with my mom, she suggested I talk with my twin brother. Perhaps he could offer me some comfort. The next day, I called and told him I needed to talk, and he said he wanted to tell me something, too. I let him go first. He told me the doctors had found a large tumor on his left testicle, and he was being tested for cancer!

I couldn't believe it. I almost didn't want to tell him that I was going through the same thing, but I did. We offered comfort to each other. A few days later when the tests came back, I was cleared of this life-threatening disease, and we planned surgery to remove the tumor.

When I talked with my brother later that day, he said his news was good, too. Although he was found to have testicular cancer, they told him it had a 100 percent cure rate, and they wanted to do his surgery right away.

I believe that we both survive today because we had a lot of prayer behind us. God gave us to each other, and I am thankful that we're still together.

Still Connected Beyond Death

That special twin bond seems to extend even beyond life on this Earth. Twins often "sense" when their co-twin meets an untimely end, may be visited by a deceased twin, and even feel the presence of a twin who didn't survive birth. Surviving twins frequently feel as if they've been cut in half when their co-twin is gone.

Dreams Lead to Discovery of Stillborn Twin
K. A. Hudson
Sydney, Australia

I had absolutely no idea that I was a twin until I turned ten years old.

When I was younger, I would have dreams every night that I was a twin, but I never felt the need to mention this to anyone. I used to dream that my twin and I would talk about everything, and laugh and play and have so much fun. I had these dreams every night up until my tenth birthday when I had a dream that was not so nice.

I dreamt that I was in a dark parking garage with my family, and my twin started running at me. I was really scared, and it frightened me. So the next morning on my tenth birthday, I told my mum about my scary dream. I also explained how I was having dreams every night that I was a twin. It was at this point that she told me I was actually once a twin! My twin was stillborn.

After that day, the twin dreams completely stopped, and I have not had one since. I miss the dreams and would still love to have them. But I believe my twin was trying to tell me about her through my dreams, and now I know the truth.

◆   ◆   ◆

Twin No Longer "Feels" His Brother
Christina
Sandston, Virginia

I was in a video-game store with my friend, Mark, who is a twin. During that time, his twin brother, Andy, got into a car accident.

There was no phone call or anything, but Mark suddenly stopped talking in the middle of his sentence. I wasn't sure what was going on in his head, but he said he had this sudden urge to go to the hospital because his brother was hurt.

As I was driving us to the hospital, Mark suddenly started to cry. When I asked what was wrong, he said he could not "feel" his brother anymore. I didn't really understand what he was talking about until we got to the hospital and found out that his brother had died.

I was really saddened by the loss of a very good and close friend. All three of us grew up together, but I thought it was amazing how far apart they were and yet Mark was able to know what had happened to his brother.

◆   ◆   ◆

I Like Being a Twin Because ...

There is always someone there you can count on without a doubt.

◆   ◆   ◆

Twin Brother Still Visits After Death
Becky
Pittsfield, Massachusetts

I am a fraternal twin. Sadly, my twin brother has been gone since 1987. He was hit by a car at age nine, and he later died in the hospital. Before he died, he told me that he wasn't going to make it. So when my family went to see him the night before he passed away, I said my good-byes. I knew it was the end, and that I would never see him again.

Even though he's been gone for nineteen years, we still have that twin connection. It's always been there, and I have a feeling it always will be. No one knew he was in the womb with me until twelve minutes after I was born, so in a sense I hid him. He was the surprise package, you could say.

One night, he broke his arm just before our last birthday together. I was at a friend's house when suddenly my arm started hurting. My friend asked me what was wrong, and I told her that I thought my twin had just broken his arm. When I got home later that evening, I found out I was right.

After his funeral, my brother came to see me, and he told me he was happy that I went to say good-bye to him. He still comes to see me once in awhile. At first it was all the time, and it would scare me as I was only nine years old. It would freak out anyone to see someone floating over them when they woke up suddenly in the middle of the night! But it doesn't frighten me anymore. He occasionally pokes me to wake me up and just say "hi." I like that my brother and I still have that "twin connection."

◆   ◆   ◆

Twin Haunted by Spirit of Dead Sister
Mel Hancock
Woongarrah, Australia

I had identical twin daughters who developed Twin to Twin Transfusion Syndrome early in my pregnancy. Around twenty-one weeks, Emma was found to be not growing, while her twin sister Elise was flourishing. An ultrasound showed Emma had major complications, which proved to be true the day of their birth.

Born nine weeks premature, it was explained or believed that during the transfusion, a blood clot had formed and lodged in Emma, stopping blood flow and causing disabilities.

On Emma's first day of life, she had major surgery on her bowel, a heart murmur, and her brain seemed to have not formed correctly.

At birth, Elise was double Emma's size and was like a newborn at the correct gestation of forty weeks in terms of her abilities. Elise was home with us at three weeks of age, but Emma had a lot of hurdles to overcome.

Sadly, after a long battle, Emma gave up and passed away at nineteen months. The moment Emma passed away, Elise woke up, and although she was only nineteen months old, Elise can tell you everything that occurred while her sister was here.

Elise is now ten years old, and over the course of her life we have witnessed what we believe to be the "twin thing." If Elise is sent to her room or for some reason is not happy, you would swear she is telling someone to the point that she will break into conversation as if she were being answered.

We moved, and Elise told us her friend was lost and couldn't find her home. When we asked her friend's name, she told us her name was Emma. She sleeps with Emma's photos inside her pillowcase.

Elise attends a Catholic school, and after a funeral was conducted at her school about three months ago, she began waking at night. She was really upset the day of the funeral so we talked about it, but she couldn't really tell why she was upset.

Now when she wakes up, she can be really hard to calm down. Once she told me she didn't want to die, and another night she told me her brother said she was going to die. I do not think this happened; I think she just thought of it herself.

Quite often when she wakes up she doesn't remember it the next day, even when she has been awake at night for up to two hours.

We have had many conversations about her sister dying, and how Emma looks after her, wants her to have the best of everything and to try to be the best person she can be. She understands all of this. I thought she was scared she was going to die like Emma, but when we talk she doesn't think she is going to die. She believes Emma is looking after her, and she is healthy, but her fears still persist.

After talking to her school and various people in professional positions, we are now thinking that Emma may be with Elise in a spirit way. Perhaps Elise talks to her and sees her, and this is scaring her. My daughter is suffering, and none of us knows how to handle it.

◆   ◆   ◆

I *Don't* Like Being a Twin Because ...

We always get compared.

◆   ◆   ◆

Twin Leads Cops to Scene of Brother's Suicide
Ian Harris
Sydney, Australia

One night, my twin brother decided to go for a ride on his motorbike. He was having marital trouble and problems at work. I was across town, 60 kilometers away, and it was late at night. His daughter called and told me he was upset and had gone for a ride.

I hopped in the car and drove across town to a beach about 100 kilometers away. I found his bike, so I slept in the car and waited for him to come back from his walk.

The cops woke me up two hours later and asked me what I was doing. I said I was waiting for my brother. They shined their flashlight in front of my car and there was my brother—washed up on the beach ... drowned.

The police told me their detectives wanted to see me and asked if I had ever been to this beach with my brother. I told them no, and explained that I was his twin. I had just had a feeling I would find him there.

◆   ◆   ◆

I Like Being a Twin Because …

We always know what is happening with each other at all times. Whether we are near each other or not, we know what is going on.

◆   ◆   ◆

Dreams of a Twin Brother Who Was Never Born
Quinn Pender
Tillamook, Oregon

From my youngest days, I always knew I'd had a twin. I knew he was male, and I called him Michael. I was born full-term, but only weighed five pounds. I have spastic cerebral palsy and fetal alcohol spectrum disorder. I was the third pregnancy for my birth mom, but the first to survive birth. My birth father died several months before I was born, and my heroic mother made the decision to give me up for adoption so I could have a better life.

I am thirty years old now. From the time I was eight years old, I would have dreams of myself and my twin, floating in a warm pink womb, kicking and playing together. I never felt like a whole person. There was always someone missing. At first I believed this was due to being adopted, but even after I met my birth mom several years ago, the feeling persisted.

The only time I have ever felt like a whole person was during my own pregnancy, which resulted in the birth of my daughter, Aaren. Sadly, my daughter was stolen from me by my adoptive parents.

I knew I'd had a twin at some point, otherwise why was I having these feelings? Why was somebody always missing? Why did I dream of Michael? My birth mom did not believe me when I suggested to her that I had been one of two. The most vivid dreams I continue to have are of my brother and I kicking each other and playing with our umbilical cords. We are laughing.

I have always been fascinated with twins, conjoined twins especially, even though Michael and I were dizygotic (developed from two fertilized ova, as fraternal twins). I now believe that Michael died in utero at the end of the first trimester, around eleven or twelve weeks. He was reabsorbed, and that is why there was no evidence of his existence. I remember him, though, and I yearn for him. I have written poems in his honor.

I have also learned that I am not the only womb twin survivor to remember their mate. I miss him. His name is Michael Eugene Holt. The more I tell the world about his tiny life, the better I feel.

◆   ◆   ◆

Brother Will Greet Twin on the "Other Side"
Richard Lees
Beaver Falls, Pennsylvania

In February 1996, I had a bad car accident in which my head hit the windshield. I was taken to the hospital. My head was stitched up, and I was sent home. Later that evening, I received a call from my twin brother who lives in another state. Before I had the opportunity to tell him about the accident, he told me he had the worst headache of his life.

When my brother was hospitalized shortly before his death, he had a brain biopsy to help determine what was wrong. The operation was done on the right side of his head. That day, I developed a large raised bump on the right side of my head. Keep in mind that we have lived apart from each other in different states for the past twenty-five years, but we have always experienced things like this throughout our lives. If one got hurt, the other felt the pain.

My twin brother, Raymond Lees, passed away on August 12, 2007. After his death, my son called me on the phone. For many people, this wouldn't seem unusual, but I had not seen my thirty-three-year-old son (and my three grandchildren) for the past five years. I had visited his last known city and searched for him, with no luck. My son was flying out east on business and came to see me. I am convinced that my twin led my son to me.

Raymond may not be with me in body, but he sure is in spirit. Twins carry that spirit inside forever. I hope to see him on the other side. I know he will be the first to greet me.

◆   ◆   ◆

Mourning a Twin Who Died at Birth
Shrishma
Vadodara, Gujarat, India

I always fantasized about having a twin. I even felt someone inside my head telling me to do things I never would have thought of. At times, I felt like I was missing half my body.

One day, while checking my files, I found a document. It said, to my shock, that I was born a twin! My sister died a few hours after the birth.

When I confronted my mom about it, the whole story came out. It was true, and they had kept it hidden from me because I was young. But they also said they didn't plan to ever tell me.

They showed me a photo of my sister and me taken directly after the birth. I always felt lonely, and now I also want to die. I feel that my life will never be complete again. I feel I am alone to face this big, bad world.

Every day, I cry in my bedroom and bathroom. People say I am too emotional because I don't have any memory of her, but I wish she was here. People don't understand the pain of losing a twin unless they have lost one.

I think it hurts more to lose a twin if you don't remember her. I will love her always and am ready to give up everything to have her back.

◆   ◆   ◆

Still Very Much a Twin
Maureen Wilkinson
Broadway, Nova Scotia, Canada

My name is Maureen, and my identical twin's name is Kathleen. Kathleen died in infancy when she was only three months old, but that doesn't make her any less my twin sister.

She has been gone now for fifty-six years and, yes, that's a long time. They say I didn't know her so I wouldn't feel the loss, but everyone is so wrong.

I think about her very much, like what it would be like to have her around, whether she would be married, have children—all those things people take for granted when they still have their twin sisters or brothers.

I know this sounds weird, but I feel her around me. There are many times when I miss her dearly and very much wish she could be here now.

My family has completely forgotten about her, but I will never forget her. Please sign me, "Still very much a twin."

◆   ◆   ◆

Waiting for a Sign from Deceased Twin
Frank Miller
Palmerton, Pennsylvania

My twin brother, Harry, passed away just two weeks ago, and I am devastated. We were also married to twin sisters, so the bond and connections between us were extremely close. I loved this guy more than words. I am waiting for some sign that he is okay. If anything like that is possible, it would happen because we were extremely close. We even thought alike. I don't think I will ever get over this.

◆   ◆   ◆

Balloons from Heaven
Kathy Dolan-Caracciola
Bayside, New York

This is about the power of love for twins even from heaven. My father, Peter Dolan, was a dedicated and adoring grandfather to his twin grandsons, Ryan and Nicholas.

Shortly after the twins turned two, my father became terminally ill. As a registered nurse and my father's only daughter, I cared for my dad until he passed. Ryan and Nicholas were there beside me every day during the course of my father's illness.

Since the day he died, every time the children acquire a balloon, whether it be from a birthday party or Applebee's, they look up to heaven as soon as they get outside and say, "Grandpa, I'm sending you another one." Then they watch the balloon disappear into the sky.

One day, after two years of sending balloons, we left Applebee's with balloons in hand. Ryan, as usual, sent his balloon up to "Granda" in heaven, but Nicholas suddenly grabbed the string in hesitation. He proceeded to give heaven the following lecture: "Listen, Granda, I've sent you like a hundred balloons, and you have never even sent me one back. Now I'm going to send you this one, but I expect you'll send one down back to me."

With that, Nicholas sent the balloon to heaven. Well, I tried to explain that it wouldn't be possible for Granda to send balloons from heaven so that Nicholas wouldn't be disappointed when he didn't receive one in return.

He told me, "Yes, he will, Mommy," and that was the last I thought of it until a week later.

My brother had just bought a new car, and he came by the house to show it to me. As I left the house, a display of eleven balloons tied together landed at my feet on the front lawn. I knew who they were from. In disbelief, I ran into the house to give them to Nicholas!

"I told you, Mommy," he said. "I told you he would send them."

Ryan looked so disappointed and asked me, "Mommy, why didn't he send me any? I asked him for some in my mind." So I tried to tell him that the balloons were to share, and with that I went back outside to my brother.

Suddenly, a second set of balloons fell from the sky and landed at my feet! You guessed it: there were eleven identical colored balloons just like the first batch. True story.

◆   ◆   ◆

I Like Being a Twin Because …

Wherever we went while growing up, people tended to pay more attention to us.

◆   ◆   ◆

Twin Lost Without Her Sister
Melissa Vinson
Homerville, Georgia

I am a surviving twin after my sister passed away five years ago. We were born in January 1970. Since her death in January 2001, my life as it was known has long left me. I have no will to live anymore, and nothing matters to me.

We were identical twins, and I feel as if someone or something took the life away from me. My whole life was shattered. To this very day, I want to die. I feel as though I can't even breathe without her. I have tried several times since she has been gone to leave this world to be with her, but the good Lord above must have a reason for me to be here because he won't let me go yet.

I am thirty-six years old, and I do not even have a place to call home. I wish there was a way I could make this feeling of longing go away, but it never ends. There are so many things that we shared that no one could even begin to understand. I just want to go home, but there's no home for me to go to. I am lost without my loving sister, Teresa, and I miss her more than anyone could ever imagine.

◆   ◆   ◆

Car Accident Separates Twins
Dalene Fouche
Worcester, Western Cape, South Africa

When my twin brother and I were twenty years old, he died in a car accident. We had a very special bond and were always together. Our twenty-first birthday was to take place on September 10. We had planned the whole party, but then he was gone. My heart is broken in pieces, and I don't know how to cope without him.

I know he is still with me and will never leave me alone, but it still doesn't take away the pain inside. Sometimes I wonder why I didn't die with him. Why am I still here on Earth while the other part of me is gone forever? People tell me everything will be okay, but they just don't understand. I just wanted to share my story so that all twins will adore their brother or sister.

◆   ◆   ◆

I *Don't* Like Being a Twin Because …

People sometimes see us as an extension of each other instead of separate people.

◆   ◆   ◆

Son Witnesses the Death of His Twin Brother
Carolyn Wilson
Birmingham, Alabama

I am the mother of eighteen-year-old, identical twin sons. On November 9, 2006, one of my sons was killed from a gunshot to the back. His brother witnessed the whole thing and held him while he was dying.

Since then, he has become angry and depressed. I know they had a special bond. They were never separated. They dressed alike even at eighteen. I hurt so deeply, but I know my son is hurting even more. I want to understand that bond even more so I can know how to help him.

Separation Anxiety

With twins, you can almost see a visible cord between them. When one's away, it's as if that cord has been severed, and they're in serious pain! They can't sleep alone, they talk on the phone constantly … they can't wait to be back together again!

Twin Feels Great Loss When Sister Moves to Ireland

Alice Babcock Lynch
Lanesborough, Massachusetts

My sister Susan and I were born fifteen minutes apart in April 1959. I was the firstborn, but have always been the smaller version of Susan. Although we are supposed to be fraternal, we have always looked alike. It was difficult for people other than our family to tell us apart. Even our boyfriends had trouble! We always had fun with that, as well as switching our classes in high school. We even have the same freckle patterns! Our mother said that we had our own language as toddlers. We have always finished each other's sentences and share the same likes and dislikes. We are both professional artists.

Much to my dismay, my twin decided to move to Ireland with her husband and their three boys. I am still heartbroken that my sister chose to live so far away from me. About six months after she moved to Ireland, I was awakened by a horrifying dream. It seemed so real to me that I woke up crying and felt like I was in shock. Up to that time, I had never been so affected by a dream.

Although it was shortly after 4:00 AM, I called and awakened my mother. Crying, I told her about the dream. I explained that in my dream I could see Susan screaming and falling backward, landing on the ground. As she was falling, she reached her arms out to me to catch her, but I could not reach her. I could feel the pain she was having. It was very real.

My mother said that I should call Susan to see if she was all right and to alleviate my fears. When I called, it was about 9:30 AM in Ireland. Much to my relief, Susan laughed and said she was fine. Nothing had happened. She said, "You just had a bad dream." We talked for awhile, and then I went back to bed.

The dream had affected me so much that I was unable to fall back to sleep. I had a very uneasy feeling that something was still very wrong. Five hours later, I received a phone call from Susan's husband. He told me that Susan was in the hospital. She had been standing on a high stool, reaching for something on a high shelf in the kitchen, when the stool went out from under her. She had fallen backward and seriously broken her back!

I don't think anyone would have believed me if I had not made the phone call after my dream. I guess I must have had some sort of premonition of her accident. Although she still lives in Ireland, we still share feelings and have the same health problems. We have a great understanding of each other, but I still feel a great loss and sadness about her decision to live so far away from me. I am very lonely because my best friend, my other self, is so far away, living her life and growing old without me. I pray every day that she will come home.

◆   ◆   ◆

I Like Being a Twin Because …

There is always someone there to talk to, to get angry at. It's like having a best friend there all the time.

◆   ◆   ◆

Twin Sleeping Beauties
Cheryl Maguire
East Bridgewater, Massachusetts

It is so easy for me to look back and realize how simple the solution was. At the time, maybe sleep deprivation was clouding my thought process.

When I first brought my boy/girl twins home from the hospital, I experienced so many different feelings. I felt excited, tired, scared, happy and, most of the time, confused.

Why are they crying?

Why won't they sleep?

What am I doing wrong?

I guess I felt that way since it seemed like all my twins did was cry, spit up and projectile vomit. It turned out they had a formula allergy. But there was also another issue that I didn't realize until they were three months old.

During the day, I would have my twins nap in the "pack and play." Since I only had one and it was so large, I had them sleep together. At night, they slept in separate bassinets in our room.

During the day, they would sleep great, sometimes for hours. At night, we were lucky if they slept for two hours. When they were awake, they would cry and cry, even after they ate. We could not figure why they slept so great during the day, but not at night. We thought of everything but the obvious answer.

Other people suggested waking them up during the day so they would sleep more at night. This did not work. They suggested having white noise since they thought that maybe the noise during the day helped them to sleep. This didn't work. They suggested having a light on at night since maybe they liked the light of the day. This also did not work.

When the twins turned three months old, their cribs finally arrived. It also seemed like a good time to transition them to their own room. They still would wake up every two hours at night so we were hesitant to have them switch rooms, but we knew it was probably the best for them. The first night, we put them in the same crib since it was so large … and they slept for eight hours! Finally, I realized why they slept so well during the day—it was because they were together!

◆   ◆   ◆

Twins Prepared to Exit the World Together
Heidi Solokis
Littleton, Colorado

I was helping my twin sister deliver her Avon orders one afternoon because she needed directions to the house of a friend of mine who lived out in the hills. As she drove, we were gabbing away when I noticed we had approached the turn-off. Then, suddenly, I said, "Oh, that's where you turn!" Almost passing it by, my sister made a quick sharp turn of the steering wheel, sending the car spinning out of control. In that instant, we thought it was going to roll! We may have screamed out in shock. I'm not quite sure. All I remember is that when the car finally came to an abrupt stop, we looked up and found ourselves with our arms wrapped around one another, and cheek to cheek. My sister must have let go of the steering wheel in panic as the car spun out of control. In total fear, we grabbed a hold of each other, preparing to die in each other's arms. After a moment of silence, we realized we were okay and right side up on a dirt road. We took one look at ourselves and started laughing hysterically at the fact that, in the moment of a life-and-death split decision, our automatic reaction was to cling to each other and die in each other's arms. We had spontaneously, without thought, prepared to go out of this world together, just as we had arrived in this world together.

◆   ◆   ◆

Twin Survey: How close are you and your twin?

We do not speak or have contact	3.1%
We talk occasionally	5.2%
No closer than typical siblings	14.6%
We are best friends	40.6%
We are inseparable	36.5%

◆   ◆   ◆

He Just Wanted to Be Near His Sister
Cassandra
Indianapolis, Indiana

Our boy/girl twins, Kennedi (my girl) and Kendall (my boy), are nearly three years old, and they are more amazing every day. They are so opposite that it's hard to find ways that they are alike, other than sleeping in tandem. Kendall is a sound sleeper and rarely wakes during the night, whereas Kennedi is a light sleeper and will get up if she hears anyone else in the house get up (even if just to go to the bathroom). After a long night of "Yes, love ... it's time for bed" and hearing "I not ready to sleep yet, Mommy ..." from Kennedi, they finally both drifted off to sleep, and I was able to finish a couple of household chores before heading to bed myself.

Later that night, I got up to get a glass of water, and I heard those familiar little footsteps coming down the stairs. Even before she reached the bottom, I said to her, "Kenni, it's okay. It's Mommy getting some water. You want some?" I got silence ... and then she burst into tears! I nearly dropped my glass. I couldn't imagine what was wrong!

When I reached the steps, there she was, sitting with her favorite naked baby doll clutched to her chest, and she said, "Mommy, I lost my Kendall!" This was too much for me to handle at 3:00 AM, so I ran up the steps, taking two steps at a time, and flung open their bedroom door, frantically looking for Kendall. I didn't see him so I started calling his name (waking everyone else in the house in the process).

I have no idea to this day what made me go back to their room to look, but I did find him … sound asleep under Kennedi's bed! They used to sleep in the same bed as infants, but the toddler beds are too small for them to sleep in together, so I assume, to Kendall, that was the closest he could get to his twin sister!

◆   ◆   ◆

Famous Mothers of Twins

Madeleine K. Albright	Loretta Lynn
Adrienne Barbeau	Martie Maguire
Angela Bassett	Mo'Nique
Meredith Baxter	Soledad O'Brien
First Lady Laura Bush	Jane Pauley
Beverly A. Cleary	Tracy Pollan
Marcia Cross	Patricia Richardson
Geena Davis	Julia Roberts
Melissa Etheridge	Emily Robison
Mia Farrow	Jane Seymour
Vonetta Flowers	Cybill Shepherd
Mia Hamm	Niki Taylor
Diana Krall	Margaret H. Thatcher
Christine Lahti	Cheryl Tiegs
Joan Lunden	

◆   ◆   ◆

Twins Separated in School Find Way to Connect
Kathy Curry
Nacogdoches, Texas

My daughters had never been separated until they started the first grade. It wasn't their first year of school, as they had attended pre-K the previous year in the same class. I had requested they be placed together again when entering first grade, but they would not allow it. Pre-K only had one class, so separating was not an option then.

On the second day of first grade, I was talking to the teacher of my youngest, Janet. She pointed out that Janet had just started crying out of the blue for her sister. The teacher thought if she took Janet and let her peek in on Brittney to see that she was okay that it would calm her down. To her surprise, Brittney was in her classroom crying for her sister as well. Brittney's teacher told Janet's teacher that she also had just started crying out of the blue right before they came to see her.

The option of letting them check on each other was left open for the rest of school year. They did well just knowing that if they needed to check on each other, they could. Fortunately, they did fine without having to do that. But they were always little chatterboxes reuniting after school!

◆   ◆   ◆

I Like Being a Twin Because …

When we were younger, I had a friend to play with.

◆   ◆   ◆

Separated for Twenty-Five Years
Tim Hall
Pembroke Pines, Florida

I have an identical twin named Tom. I am three minutes older, but he's been about an inch taller and about ten pounds heavier since we were teenagers. We are now in our late forties. We dressed alike until we were in high school, and we even looked quite a bit alike. We were inseparable.

When we were in our early twenties, however, he moved away when he was transferred by his employer, Kay Jewelers. At that point, I wasn't sure what I wanted to do with my life yet, so I figured if Tom was happy at Kay Jewelers, then I would be happy there, too! I started with them in 1981 on our twenty-second birthday (May 26). I even met my wife, Stephanie, whom I've been married to for twenty years, in a Kay Jewelers store in Burlington, Iowa. She was my boss (and still is!), and I was her assistant manager.

Over the course of the next ten to twelve years, Tom and I were busy building our careers, which meant that he would be in one state and I would be in another. In the past twenty-five years, we've been lucky if we got to spend one week a year together. There were times when we would go two to three years without seeing each other.

Nevertheless, Tom and I are still extremely close in our hearts, even though we've been 1,300 miles apart. He lives in Indiana, while I live in South Florida. We often think of calling each other when the phone rings and it's the other person.

I'm sure there are many other twins who have been separated by careers and desperately want to be closer again. About four years ago, I created a greeting card for twins to give each other to express the closeness that twins have. I was hoping that by starting a greeting card line for twins and by sharing our story that my brother and I could somehow get back together and share so many of the things that we have lost over the years. So far, that hasn't happened, but hopefully it will some day.

◆   ◆   ◆

Separation Is Short-Lived
Courtney
Boise, Idaho

My twin cousins, Bob and Ellen, are a few years younger than me. They grew up in Ohio, and I grew up in California.

They used to come out to visit when we were little. I had a big drawer of dress-up clothes, and Ellen and I always wanted to play house. Of course, Bob never wanted to be left out, so he would play, too. But he took "not being left out" to a whole new level!

He was the only boy, but he wasn't going to let that stop him. He always had to be the mom. I had this tacky fake pearl handbag he loved so much that my mom made me give it to him. For a long time, he took that purse everywhere ... and I mean everywhere! My aunt still talks about all the funny looks she got at the store when they were kids.

A few years back, my cousins were separated for the first time at the age of twenty-five. He went to Washington, and she was in West Virginia. It didn't last. They now both live in South Carolina!

◆   ◆   ◆

I *Don't* Like Being a Twin Because ...

We can't cope when we're apart.

◆   ◆   ◆

Hand-in-Hand Twins
Marisa Berquist
Rockland, Maryland

I had boy/girl twins in April 2006. Lily came home with me after my C-section, but Cole stayed in the NICU for an extra week. Lily cried when he was gone and didn't sleep well. On the night Cole came home from the hospital, I was holding both of them on my chest, and they started holding hands. Every night from then on, they have grabbed each other's hand and held it while they slept. They still do it even at fifteen months old!

◆　　◆　　◆

Twins Only Sleep Well with Each Other
Tina Wells
Cocoa, Florida

The first time I noticed my twins' bond was when they were three months old. We had to put Laci in the hospital for a week because of a very bad infection. That was the first time since they were born that they had slept apart. I stayed at the hospital with Laci, and my husband and mother-in-law stayed home with Lexis.

When they came to visit each morning, we seemed to have the same complaint: neither girl was sleeping at all. After about two days, it was safe to bring Lexis to visit her sister. As soon as she arrived, we placed her in the hospital crib with Laci. They both reached out their hands until they were touching one another, and then promptly went to sleep.

They slept for four or five straight hours, never moving away from each other. To this day, they can't sleep if one isn't in the house. And even though they fight like cats and dogs, one will not leave the house without the other.

◆　　◆　　◆

Twins Fight, but Still Miss Each Other
Annalee Frazee
Fontana, California

I have twin girls who will be two years old in three months. They are always fighting, pulling hair, biting, hitting, and telling each other "no." One of them is more of a bully than the other, but when they are away from each other, they ask for the other. They are very much the same, but are also very different. One is loud, rough and tough; the other is whiny and more of a girly-girl.

◆   ◆   ◆

I Like Being a Twin Because ...

I can always tell what my twin is thinking and feeling.

◆   ◆   ◆

Continents Separate Twins
Lena

I have a twin sister, but we live on two different continents. Sometimes I feel bad for being the one who left because since I have moved to Europe, my sister has been having difficulties with her weight. I know that her weight issues have to do with the fact that we live so far apart, but I have to complete my studies before I can go back, and that will be in three years.

When we were younger, we invented our own language, and we have a sense of humor that only we get. I am the smaller one, and for some reason I have always been the one who got into trouble for stuff my sister did. Even my mother used to mistake me for my sister.

When we were in high school, we had to write a fictional diary spanning over a week. We could add drawings to the text if we wanted to, and it turned out that we wrote the same fictional stories and also did the exact same drawings. We did not get the ideas from childhood storybooks. They were completely made-up stories!

Both of us want to have children, but neither of us seems to get pregnant even though we are fertile. I reckon it will probably only happen at the same time or not at all.

◆   ◆   ◆

The Half That Makes Her Whole

Jennifer Harwood
Grace, Idaho

My identical twin sister and I were born five minutes apart. My sister, Janet, was born first, and I came out holding onto her ankle. I guess I didn't want her leaving without me.

When we were fourteen years old, my sister got Hodgkin's disease. I spent many days by her hospital bed for fear that something would happen to her and I wouldn't be there. She was in the hospital for about five weeks, and when she finally got to come home, I was the only one she trusted to clean her broviack (a tube that they put into her chest so they could give her chemo). I sat by her side many times while she was having her chemo. It broke my heart to see her so sick, but I wouldn't have been anywhere else.

When we were seventeen years old, I became pregnant. Like all teenagers, my sister and I fought a lot. I remember my sister telling me that she couldn't wait until I got married so I could move out and she wouldn't have to see me anymore. She even told me that she wasn't going to miss me.

We lived in a small town in Southeast Idaho, and as soon as I got married, I moved to Nampa, Idaho, which is about five hours away from my sister. I cried all the way to Nampa because I missed her so much! The day after I moved, I got a phone call from … guess who? My beloved twin sister. She called to tell me she was sorry, and that she missed me already. She wanted to know when I was coming to see her.

Since that day, I have talked to my twin sister every single day! We usually stay on the phone for at least an hour. Our husbands still don't understand how we can talk to each other every day for hours on end and never run out of stuff to talk about. She is my sister and my best friend, and this world would be a very lonely place without her in my life.

I guess it is true what they say: "Absence makes the heart grow fonder." My sister's cancer has been in remission for sixteen years now. She has two children, and I have five. If anything ever happened to her, I would be right there by her side. She is the half that makes me whole, and I will love her forever and always!

◆   ◆   ◆

Twins Share Punishments!
Heather
Oregon City, Oregon

When my twin sister, Hillary, and I were growing up, I was the troublemaker. When I would be sent to our room, Hillary would tell my mom that she was also bad so she could be sent to our room, too. She would beg and beg to be sent to our room just because she wanted to be with me. But our mom always knew the truth and wouldn't let her!

◆   ◆   ◆

I *Don't* Like Being a Twin Because ...

People sometimes resented that we got extra attention.

◆   ◆   ◆

Nothing Will Come Between Them
Sandi Tunnard
Greenwell Sprints, Louisiana

My name is Sandi Reneé Tunnard, and I have a twin sister named Brandi Deneé Tunnard. We are very close and have been our whole lives. Brandi was born at 10:19 AM and I was born at 10:20 AM on August 13, 1982.

The bond that my twin sister and I have is strong and always will be. We finish each other's sentences, say the same things at times, feel when the other is in some kind of trouble, and talk for hours about silly things. My twin sister and I have been inseparable since we were born, but just recently we moved fifty miles from each other.

I miss my sister so much because we did everything together. We slept in the same bed growing up, and we even shared boyfriends at times!

I am thankful that the Lord blessed my mother with twins. Brandi means the world to me, and without her I would be incomplete. No one will ever come between us.

Teenage Twins

Getting through adolescence is frequently like riding a roller coaster—filled with many ups and downs—but twin teens often feel fortunate to have a sibling along to share the ride. They may start growing apart and no longer be carbon copies of each other, but they still find that the "twin connection" stays strong throughout the teen years.

Scottish Twins Are Two Parts of a Whole
Denise and Heather Allan
Scotland

As with a lot of twins, we share a bond like no other. We are twins, sisters, friends, teachers and mirrors for each other. We are fifteen years old, identical and have only lived one minute without each other (at birth).

We speak to each other in a language no one else can understand, nor can we enlighten them. We didn't realize this until we were six or seven years old when someone pointed it out. It involves using the same number of syllables, but making a different noise. It can be useful in class, letting each other know how we feel or what we are thinking. Of course, that is the verbal way of doing so. In a situation when we are being asked to do something (e.g., being asked to go out with friends), we know the exact excuse (genuine or not) for not doing so within a matter of seconds, with no expression or sound.

Other times, we start talking about the exact same thing at the exact same time. More frequently, when telling a story or having a conversation, we finish each other's sentences. For example, once when we were shopping, we both said the same thing at the same time, and then responded at the same time with the same answer. This went on for several minutes.

This is not the only way we understand each other's thoughts and feelings. The first occurrence of experiencing each other's pain was when we were eight years old. Denise broke her elbow. Walking slowly home from where it had happened, Heather was crippled with pain in the opposite arm. Not only was this one of many times we have experienced unexplainable pain, but we have also experienced visible changes.

At age ten, Heather visited the dentist, anxious of the awaiting jag to remove her tooth. At home, Denise experienced a similar numbness and looked in the mirror to investigate. On the opposite side of her mouth, above the same tooth, Denise's gum was bleeding.

In March of this year, Heather was diagnosed with Type 1 diabetes. She spent a week in hospital, which is the first time we had slept without each other. When Heather came home, now injecting three times a day, Denise refused to eat anything Heather could not eat. Getting used to this unfamiliar routine, Heather was checking her blood sugar regularly (pricking her finger and inserting it into a monitor), and she was left with hundreds of tiny purple bruises on her fingertips. After a week or two, Denise bore the same marks, in the same places.

Our memories are also different from other people's. We remember with great detail and clarity what the other experienced. For example, we both remember taking the rubbish out on holiday. Only one of us did this, yet we both remember the squirrel on the fence.

Our extraordinary bond is also reflected in our achievements academically. It is a constant competition to achieve the highest marks, and therefore our education has benefited. Our teachers and friends know us as "The Allans," "The Girls" or simply "The Twins." Some believe this to affect our individualism and confidence. However, we are proud to be known collectively because we are two parts of a whole!

10 Reasons We Love Being Twins

1. The eternal companionship

2. The spooky moments

3. All the attention!

4. Our school grades

5. The nightly sleepovers

6. The privacy of our language

7. The unquestionable understanding

8. The unbreakable trust

9. The undeniable continuous task of pleasing one another

10. All those disastrous moments (especially baking, aka burning!)

Not actually in that order … they are all number one!!!

◆   ◆   ◆

I *Don't* Like Being a Twin Because …

We get the same gift on our birthdays.

◆　　◆　　◆

Absence Makes Twins' Hearts Grow Fonder
Amanda
Toronto, Ontario, Canada

My brother and I are fraternal twins, ten minutes apart, and very different indeed. When we were younger, we couldn't stand each other. We'd get in both verbal and physical fights; no one could stop us.

As we grew older, the fighting stopped, but without the fighting we were left with pretty much nothing to say to each other. Sure, at times we'd have a laugh or go down to the park to get ice cream, but it was all just skin-deep. I know that we both love each other deep down inside, but we've never really bonded.

Last year, my mother sent me off to a boarding school in Toronto, while my brother stayed behind. It hurt a lot knowing that we wouldn't see each other, and that there'd be a twelve-hour difference. Still, we managed to talk on the phone or e-mail if we weren't too busy.

This year, I spent my first birthday without him (my sweet 16th). It didn't feel right. After all, we usually blew out the candles and cut the cake together. This time, my birthday wish was to always have close contact with him, no matter what.

A few months later, I was sick with the flu. My mother called and told me my brother had the flu as well. Another time, I hurt my toe while in gym class and couldn't walk properly for a week; my brother hurt his toe in the exact same place while playing soccer with his friends the same day.

It could be coincidental, but at times in random moments I'll feel an overwhelming emotion to call him up just to see if he's okay. He's told me more than once that he was glad I called; he needed someone to talk to. He's opening up a lot more now, and keeps me up-to-date on the comings and goings of my friends back home.

It seems silly to wish on your birthday to be closer to your twin, but I'm glad I admitted to myself that I did not want to lose contact with him after all. Now we're even closer than before. I guess it is true that absence makes the heart grow fonder.

◆   ◆   ◆

Twin Survey: Do you and your twin dress alike?

We always dress alike	16.2%
We sometimes dress alike	28.3%
We never dress alike	10.1%
We used to dress alike when we were younger, but we no longer do	36.4%
Other	9.1%

◆   ◆   ◆

Best Friends 4 Ever
Nicole
Sewell, New Jersey

My name is Nicole. I have a twin sister named Natalie, and we are fifteen years old. I love her to death. We never fight; we have the same friends; we go to dance school together; we pretty much do everything together. It is so fun being a twin because you always have someone there to talk to who knows exactly what you're going through.

We are more than best friends. It's a bond that no one can explain. Only twins know what I'm talking about. I would do anything for her. In school, we could be in different classes, but still think and talk alike. For instance, I asked my friend something and she answered me, and a couple of minutes later my sister aggravated her by asking the same question! We found out later and laughed about it.

First days of school are always fun for us. We go to our separate classes, and our teachers don't know that we are twins until they go to say hello to the wrong one and wonder why we didn't answer them.

Being a twin always attracts stares. One time when we were out to dinner with our family at a restaurant, we went to get our food at the buffet, and everyone just stared at us like they had never seen twins before. We looked at each other and started laughing. It was so funny. We felt like celebrities! People constantly look twice when they pass us by, but never before did we have such a big crowd of people staring at us as we did in the restaurant.

The weird and unexplainable connections that twins have never get old. Every day, something new happens to us, and we are only fifteen. We still have our whole lives ahead of us, and our bond can only get stronger. BEST FRIENDS 4 EVER.

◆   ◆   ◆

Shopping with a "Twin Twist"
Theresa Conley
Demorest, Georgia

One evening, my family, consisting of six children plus parents, went to Wal-Mart for a shopping adventure. We were all allowed to venture out on our own as long as we met back at a specific time and place.

I walked around the store with my identical twin for the majority of the time, but we eventually parted company.

When it came time for the family to gather at the front of the store, my sister didn't show. While my family paged her and waited up front, I was given permission to quickly run through the store to see if I could spot her.

I was aggravated and worried as I looked past clothing racks and started to check the aisles, when I caught a glimpse of her. I turned around, stood at the end of the aisle, and proceeded to cuss her out. "Jennifer, where have you been?! I have been looking everywhere for you!" Noticing that she was performing the same exaggerated movements I was, I got even angrier and said, "Stop doing that!"

Then I caught the eye of a bewildered customer and took inventory of the situation. I could feel my face turn red, and I ran from the area when I discovered that I was looking at my own reflection in a mirror that had been placed at the end of the aisle.

When I reached the front of the store, my sister and family were waiting on me. I didn't tell them what had happened until after we left. When they heard my story, everyone busted out laughing and teased me for weeks.

◆   ◆   ◆

I Like Being a Twin Because ...

We can swap places.

◆   ◆   ◆

Twin Teenagers Talk About Their Bond
Christine and Kristina Vi
Arlington, Virginia

Christine:

Kristina and I have connections that go on and off randomly. It happens very quickly for a couple of seconds. On one occasion, we were going to walk to an art supply store so that I could pick up a sketchbook. As I was stepping out of the house, I felt a pinch, like a needle pricking my heart. The next day, when we were cooking in the kitchen, I knew I had to talk to Kristina about it.

"Kristina, when we were stepping out the door yesterday to walk to the store, did you feel a sharp pain?" I said.

Kristina stared at me for a moment and then replied, "Yeah. Uh-huh." I knew this was the twin telepathy thing, so I questioned her again.

"Where did you feel it?" Kristina placed her hand on her heart, and I got the chills! It was the same spot!

I told her, "That's where I had it, too!"

"Really?" she said. "Cool! It's Twin Telepathy!"

Kristina and I want to show everyone the special bond and uniqueness of having a twin. A lot of people think that when you're a twin, you have the advantage of being able to switch places. That's true since Kristina and I have done it before, but that's not all there is to being a twin. Being a twin has its responsibilities. You have to respect, trust, and support the other no matter the situation because your twin is a piece of you, and without the "other you," you wouldn't be a whole.

Kristina:

Christine is my one-minute-older twin sister. We share everything, from rooms to television. Our connection is weak, but it is increasing. We can sometimes read each other's minds, finish each other's sentences, and pretty much order the same food in restaurants. Sometimes, Christine and I will get the same thoughts or ideas, but they may vary in little ways. We do not always agree, but we agree on most things. We've been through tough times together, but managed to survive it all. Christine is my best, most truest, and only friend.

◆   ◆   ◆

Famous Female Twins

Karen Black	Ann Landers & Abigail Van Buren
Brittany and Cynthia Daniel	Alanis Morissette
Ann B. Davis	Tia and Tamera Mowry
Deidre Hall	Mary-Kate and Ashley Olsen
Linda Hamilton	Alexandra Paul
Heloise (the original)	Isabella Rossellini
Jill Hennessy	Jean and Liz Sagal
Scarlett Johansson	

◆   ◆   ◆

Teen Marriage Separates Twins
Brandie
Vian, Oklahoma

My twin sister, Brittany, and I have been so close all our lives, like any other set of twins. We did everything together, like peanut butter and jelly. We were hardly ever apart. But when we turned seventeen, Brit moved out and got married!

It's been almost a year now, and I'm still pretty bummed about it. It's hard not getting to see her, and some days we don't even talk. We both have different schedules, and it makes me sad.

We went from being together every day, all day long, to talking maybe three or four times a week. I could use some advice on how to get through this!

◆   ◆   ◆

I Like Being a Twin Because …

Someone knows what it is like being me and understands what I go through on a daily basis.

◆   ◆   ◆

Twins Are Total Opposites!
Elizabeth Leigh Kohnen
Highlands Ranch, Colorado

My twin brother and I are juniors at different high schools. People think it is bizarre that we are twins because we look nothing alike and our personalities are totally opposite. While I look more like my mom with brown/red hair and green eyes, Eric looks more like my dad, except that he has blond hair and blue eyes.

He makes straight A's; I've been diagnosed with learning disabilities. He is quiet, and I am loud. We are totally opposite except for two things: we are each other's best friend, and our smiles are exactly the same. When we were small, instead of a security blanket or a teddy bear, I had Eric. When Mommy or Daddy weren't there, as long as Eric was, I was fine. Not a lot has changed since then.

We recently went to an auction and raffle drawing at a charity event. Eric and I both had tickets for the raffle, but our numbers were all off because I had showed up to the event an hour earlier than Eric. Several items were raffled off until the last item was up: a $20 gift certificate to Olive Garden. They called a number, and Eric and I, sitting next to each other, both sat up, looked at the stage, and then looked at each other. We both smiled and held up our tickets. As I reflect back on this, I bet everybody was wondering what we were doing! When comparing the tickets, we realized that Eric had the number they called, and my number was the same number, but in reverse order. Eric and I went onstage, got our gift certificate, and ate together at Olive Garden the next weekend.

When looking through family videos, I realize that our relationship hasn't changed at all considering how much we've grown up. We're still the little kids tackling and biting each other, like two little puppies, but now we're two sixteen-year-olds acting like idiots. And none of this changes the fact that I love my brother.

◆   ◆   ◆

Twin Hears Sister's Silent Call
Christine Vi
Arlington, Virginia

I'm not a huge fan of the mall, but there was a particular day that changed my opinion. My twin sister, Kristina, had separated from me since we wanted to go to different stores. We always met up at Forever XII, but when I got there, Kristina hadn't arrived, so I had to wait. I walked around the store to see if I could find my mother, which I did.

I still had trouble locating Kristina, and I remember turning in different directions wondering where she was. My mind was saying: "Where are you? Where are you?"

All of a sudden, a familiar, perky face come around the corner of the store and greeted me. Kristina had found her way to me. She told me she had "heard" the call.

Well, I'm not a huge fan of phones or talking. In fact, I don't even own a cell phone. Kristina told me she had heard me "calling" her in her mind. I was very happy to hear this as I didn't even need a phone to do what I just did!

Kristina and I think this is a really cool way to communicate. We hope it happens more often and that we can begin to talk to each other without actually talking. It would be nice to have someone to tell you the answers on a test, don't you think?

◆   ◆   ◆

I *Don't* Like Being a Twin Because ...

She wears my clothes!

◆   ◆   ◆

Teenage Twins Grow Apart
Kelley Call
Hansen, Idaho

My twin sister, Kylie, is one minute younger than me, and we both turned six-teen on May 31, 2006. Many times, we'll be thinking the same things, even the most random thoughts. It's funny sometimes because we'll just be hanging out with our friends, and we'll start singing a song at the same time out of nowhere. It kind of freaks them out.

Kylie and I used to be really close. For our younger years, we only had each other as friends, and we shared absolutely everything with each other. But then we entered junior high. I became a little more independent from her and wanted to hang out with other people more often. Since then, we've been more and more distant from each other. The weird part is that both of us are changing. Our thoughts, which used to be nearly identical to each other, are now entirely differ-ent. I know it's tearing my sister up inside that I've begun to spend more time with my other friends and less with her.

Sometimes I just feel like she's smothering me, wanting to be with me every second, but I still love her very much, and she loves me the same as always. This connection we have will keep us sharing a bond that a lot of sisters, and especially twins, are very lucky to experience.

I know she's feeling left out and sad that we are going through different changes, and I hope she knows I still care for her as much as I did before, and per-haps even more. We'll never forget each other. We even still have the same dreams every once in a while! Anyway, I still love you, Sis! And you know I always will.

◆   ◆   ◆

The M&M Brothers
Michael and Manuel Cordova
Tucson, Arizona

Michael:

My twin and I are so close that we both wrote a twin story on this website today. I guess you could say my twin and I are exactly the same. We do everything together. We dress the same without telling each other what we are going to wear. When my twin and I were both five years old, Manuel went with his little friend to Patagonia Lake in Nogales. While he was up there, he fell and hit his head right on top of his right eyebrow and had seven stitches. On that exact same day, I also hit my head on a table and had to get seven stitches, too. We were both scarred in the exact same spot!

On May 20, 2001, my twin brother had back surgery for a broken bone in his back from a fall onto his butt that smashed a bone. When they took him back to get him ready for surgery, I could feel him panicking because of his fright, and I started freaking out. I had to get examined to see what was wrong with me, and the doctor told my parents that I could feel my brother's pain.

The next day when my brother awoke and tried to get up, he was in severe pain, and I could feel it. The doctor set us next to each other, and he pushed on my brother's incision. I screamed in pain for him to stop.

That was the day I found out that my twin and I were closer than I thought. We could actually feel each other's pain. Since then, we do everything together. Hopefully, we will be able to write a book about our lives and how it is to be a twin who can feel each other's pain.

Manuel:

My brother and I are both eighteen years old, and we are identical twins. My twin brother and I have a strong bond together. We are always with each other no matter what. When we go to malls or clothing stores, we always buy the same clothes. When we get dressed, we try and dress differently from each other, but we end up dressing the same. That's how close we are.

We sometimes pretend we are looking in a mirror and make our friends laugh because we imitate each other. Our parents can't really tell us apart, so they call us M&M since both our names start with "M."

When we are apart, I can tell if there is something wrong back home because I get headaches and really bad stomachaches. The headaches are a sign that something happened in the family. The stomachaches mean my twin has hurt himself. So the minute I feel them, I am on the phone before you know it, any time of the day.

In high school, my twin and I worked at the same jobs and had the same classes together, so we were around each other almost 24/7. We have the same car, phones, pets, everything. At the mall, some people stare at us because they see two identical people walking together. Some people are ashamed of being a twin because they have someone who looks like them, but my brother and I are very proud of looking exactly the same.

No twins should hate each other. All twins have a bond, and nothing can ever change that. My twin and I have never been in a fight with each other because we usually agree with each other's thoughts, and if we don't we choose what we like better. I am proud to say that I have an identical twin who is always by my side.

◆   ◆   ◆

I Like Being a Twin Because …

Chicks dig it.

◆   ◆   ◆

Twins Bonded by Croup
Danielle Sandall
Lynnwood, Washington

My name is Danielle, and I'm a fraternal twin. I'm sixteen years old, and my twin sister is four minutes older than me.

One day after school, my sister was going outside, and I was in another room away from her. All of a sudden, I felt this sharp pain in my finger, and I went to our mom crying. About two minutes later, my sister showed up crying; she had slammed her finger in the door! I felt it before it happened to her.

When I was six years old, I got the croup, which is an illness that attacks the lungs and heart and can kill. My sister was sleeping on the top bunk, and I was sleeping on the bottom. She was sleeping soundly when I woke her up in a panic because I couldn't breathe. She told me to go back to bed because she didn't realize I wasn't okay. I went to my mom's room and pounded on the door over and over, but my mom kept saying, "Hold on, sweetie." I couldn't hold on because I was running out of time. My grandma heard the commotion, ran to my mom's room, and yelled as loudly as she could, "Your daughter is blue. She needs to go to the hospital!" While my mom got the car ready, my twin sister came out of our room crying. She said, "Dani, I love you. Don't go now. I need you still." After the treatment was over and I went home, I asked my sister what that was about. She said, "I had a dream that you were really sick and were going to die. I didn't want you to die because you are a part of me."

Ever since that day, my sister and I have been inseparable. We share everything and make decisions based on each other. Every date, plans, or get-together, we are both there. My twin is my best friend.

◆   ◆   ◆

Brother's Cancer Devastates Twin
Tyson Gerald
San Francisco, California

Nathaniel, my twin, who I called Nat or Nattier, was never what you'd call the strongest person in the world. When he was fourteen, he stopped eating breakfast, and then other meals. I was the only one really noticing, and I was terrified. I asked him what was wrong, but he said it was nothing. He told me he had been eating when he got home from school. (I have basketball practice after school, and he was home alone for two hours a day.)

After about a week, I noticed that he had lost a whole lot of weight—I mean, a lot, in just one little week. Nat had been through a stage in life where he was depressed. It was actually worse than most teenage cases of depression. When he was thirteen, I caught him just before he killed himself. Our parents sent him to therapy, and he got better, but the fact that he was not eating made me scared that he was depressed again. I was very, very wrong.

One morning, I woke up because my stomach hurt a little bit. Now, my brother and I feel each other's pain sometimes, but I thought that the pain was mine, not his. It was getting really late, and Nat hadn't woken up, so I tried to shake him. He said that his stomach hurt so bad he didn't want to get up.

I told my parents that he was sick and was not going to school, and then I left. I skipped practice and went home to see if he was okay. I was with him for a few minutes, and then he started to throw up blood.

I called an ambulance, and right after I did, Nat passed out from weakness after throwing up half his stomach. When the doctor said that he had stomach cancer, and it had progressed very far in his body, I was crushed.

My parents arranged for chemo right away. Nattie didn't take the chemo very well. After the first few days, he landed in the ICU with a really bad fever. On his third time in the ICU, the doctors said he wasn't expected to live. They also said that if he did, he couldn't go back on chemo because his immune system was proving to be very weak.

I was with him when he died. God almighty, I don't even want to think about how sick he looked. Sweating and trembling and all that. He just died. I don't want to get into our last conversation, or what I said to him while he was sick. He died, though. Dead. Gone.

◆   ◆   ◆

Teen Twins Are Best Friends
Christine Vi
Arlington, Virginia

I love being a twin because ...

1. We have SUPER TWIN POWERS!

2. There is always someone who can switch places with you between classes.

3. If you want to know how good you look in an outfit, hairstyle, etc., you can look to your twin as a model.

4. Your twin is your BEST FRIEND!!!

5. Your twin is the only person who is there for you when you need someone to talk to.

Two Heads Are Better Than One

There's a reason why they call twins "double trouble." With two minds working together, they can do some serious damage to the house, finish each other's sentences, and stick up for each other. Even twins with different strengths and weaknesses frequently have a synchronicity that comes in handy!

Twin Trick or Treat!
Heidi Solokis
Littleton, Colorado

My identical twin sister and I were born on Halloween in 1964, four minutes apart. Audrey was born first, and I came second. Therefore, she was the "trick" and I was the "treat"! We weighed in at four pounds each, arriving six weeks early. My mother named Audrey after Audrey Hepburn, and my father named me Heidi (a German name because we were born in Germany).

We were "army brats." My father was serving in the army and married my mother, a beautiful young German woman. They had been married two years before our birth. We were affectionately called "Pumpkin" by our father. A lot of our birthday parties were costume parties, and we always had pumpkin pie for birthday cake—our favorite!

When we were in the third grade, our little friends talked us into playing a "trick" on our teachers. We had the pod set-up at grade school (one big area divided into four classrooms). Audrey and I switched seats after recess one day and were in classrooms that were diagonal from each other. Audrey's teacher asked me a question on a subject I had not taken yet. (The classes rotated during the day on different lessons.) All of the kids were giggling, watching the "big switcharoo" in action. Startled that the teacher had called upon me, I giggled nervously, got up, and walked over to my assigned seat. Audrey went back to hers. The teachers and children laughed at the little prank, and we enjoyed the attention.

We pulled another "trick" in high school, this one involving dates we had for a Saturday night. We were eighteen years old and best friends with another set of identical twins, who were seventeen years old. Their names were Karen and Kelly. I had a date with Marty, a guy I had seen a few times already. Kelly had a date with Frank, and it was their second date. Karen and Audrey answered the door when our dates arrived, and pretended to be "Kelly and Heidi," ready to go out. My date sat down and visited with Audrey, kind of confused at why she was there. (Kelly and I were hiding behind the wall divider, watching this all play out.) Frank, Kelly's date, after a brief conversation, suddenly leaned over to kiss Karen hello, and that's when Karen freaked out. She leaned back to sway away from the kiss, saying, "Oh no, I'm Karen!" Kelly and I came around the wall divider into the front room and claimed our confused dates, laughing hysterically. We hadn't fooled Marty, but we sure got Frank good! It was so funny, and a great story to tell all of our friends!

Audrey and I are forty-two years old now, and we're still best friends—closer than close. We always have been, and always will be. And we do still have a few "tricks" up our sleeves!

◆　　◆　　◆

Twin Interpreters
Charmaine Hardie
Pietermaritzburg, South Africa, Natal

I am the mother of eight-year-old fraternal twin boys who are extremely close. They are in different classes, and when I fetch them from school, I do not even bother to talk to them for the first five minutes as they are so busy "re-connecting." I also have an older boy, and they are all very close, but there is a definite bond between the twins.

When they were just learning to talk, Twin A (Christopher) was desperately trying to tell me something while traveling in the car, repeating the same (indistinct) word over and over. I kept trying different words ("Do you mean …?"), but could not figure out what he was saying.

Twin B (Andrew) sat very quietly until we drove past my older son's school. Then he pointed to the school and very loudly (as if I was stupid) repeated the same indistinct word. When I asked if that word meant "Michael" (my older son's name), they both smiled broadly and said yes!

Andrew obviously knew all along what Christopher had meant, but just bided his time until he could "explain" it to me! Although they do not have a "twin language," they clearly understand each other. Their speech has improved a hundredfold, but they still attend speech therapy.

◆　　◆　　◆

Sisters Connect Through a Locked Door
Vladi Hobbs
Calgary, Alberta, Canada

My identical twin girls, Adrianna and Breanna, were twenty months old. It was one of those days when the girls just weren't getting along … whatever one had, the other one wanted.

So when the hair-pulling began, I placed the younger of the two (by four minutes), Breanna, in time-out for about a minute in their room. I closed the door so that she could not lash out and get her sister.

Unfortunately, instead of it being just one minute, it turned into twenty minutes. I did not realize that my little goober could reach the door handle, so when she tried to get out she accidentally locked herself in the room! I discovered this when I went to get her out and could not open the door.

Then, of course, panic set in. Breanna was crying. Adrianna, at this point, still just thought her sister was in tears because she was in trouble, so she thought nothing of it.

But as soon as I started to jiggle the handle and tried to calm down Breanna, Adrianna perked up as if she sensed that something was wrong. She ran over and started babbling to the bedroom door and hugging it.

It was like she knew something was wrong. Once I realized that I could not get in, I called my neighbor's husband to help, and he came over to drill out the lock. By this time, Breanna was freaking out.

Once she started to cry, Adrianna pressed herself to the door on her side and, through her tears, started babbling back to her sister. It brought tears to my eyes, too.

We did eventually get the lock out, but before we did we were able to squeeze my six-year-old son through the window to calm Breanna down. Once the door opened, Adrianna ran to her sister, hugged her, and brought her to me. Then they both sat on my lap, hugging and crying together, for about fifteen minutes.

I will never know what they were thinking, but it was amazing to see Adrianna run to her sister, knowing she was in trouble even at such a young age.

◆   ◆   ◆

I *Don't* Like Being a Twin Because ...

People always stop us and want to ask questions.

◆   ◆   ◆

Twins' Personalities Are Complementary
Susan Hegvold
Healdsburg, California

I didn't know I was having twins when Erik and Katrina were born. I had a homebirth with midwives, and even though I was abnormally large, we didn't think too much of it because I was big with my first daughter, and this was a second pregnancy after all. I didn't realize there was another baby in there until after I had given birth to Erik and Katrina popped out! She was still in her amniotic sac with her eyes open. It was very magical.

My twins are now twelve years old. I don't know the extent of their inner connection yet, but I do know that they actually enjoy each other's company very much. My son, Erik, is the comedian in the family, and my daughter, Katrina, is a more introspective and dreamy personality. She says that it is her curse in life to always laugh at Erik's jokes, no matter how lame they may be.

My husband has said that it's like Erik is living in a cartoon world complete with pratfalls and sound effects. I do know there is a definite connection between the two of them, but it is almost a synchronistic relationship in that they go their own way and come together at times, complementing each other with their own strengths and talents. They get along very well, but a lot of that has to do with Katrina's easygoing nature.

Erik is like fireworks going off, brilliant and dazzling at times, and then on to the next project. Katrina is persevering and steady, and astonishes us with her accomplishments over time. I can imagine them working well together in some sort of career—Erik the idea man and Katrina patiently working with his ideas to make them come together.

◆   ◆   ◆

What Do Twins, Coke, and Cereal Have in Common?
Robin Bentley
Clay, New York

I have always had a close bond with my twin sister, Buffie. We went to the same college, worked at the same supermarket during college, and have both been working at the same financial company for the last eight years (in different departments).

My sister Buffie is married with two kids. She and her husband met on a blind date around seven years ago. I have a wonderful boyfriend, and he and I met on a blind date a little over two years ago.

One of our favorite twin stories to tell is about one morning when we were in eighth grade. I came downstairs to have breakfast, and I poured some cereal in a bowl. Then I grabbed some Coke from the refrigerator and was just about to pour it into my cereal when I realized that I had grabbed the Coke instead of the milk!

My dad had witnessed the whole thing, and it gave him a chuckle. Then I poured in the milk, ate my cereal, and went back upstairs to finish getting ready for school. While I was upstairs, I heard my dad laughing really loud. I poked my head down the stairs and asked what was so funny. He said that my twin sister had just poured Coke in her cereal! He couldn't believe that I had almost made such a silly mistake, and then my sister came down later and did the same thing (but didn't catch herself before pouring).

My sister and I are closer to each other than any other sisters I know. Our personalities are identical, our interests are identical, and we always think the same way!

◆   ◆   ◆

I Like Being a Twin Because ...

She would never let me down nor would I let her down. We can totally count on each other.

◆   ◆   ◆

Twin Prank Delivers Big Laughs
Brian Roberts
Ontario, Canada

I am the other half of a set of identical twins. My twin brother is Dave, and we were born in the small town of Tillsonburg back in 1958, when identical twins were rare. They even put it in the paper back then. I can honestly say it has been an amazing life experience being an identical twin.

I don't know if our parents did it to torture the rest of the family, but they dressed us exactly the same until we were nine years old. Nobody could tell us apart except our mom. One thing we both hated was our relatives making us stand side by side to see if they could tell us apart. They could never get it right, and when they did, we told them they were wrong anyway just for fun. Even to this day, people get us mixed up. When I am shopping, I'll run into people all the time, and they will walk up and say, "Hi, Dave. How are you doing?" Sometimes I will correct them and tell them I am Brian.

When we were young, we were the holy terrors of the neighborhood. What one didn't think of, the other one did. I remember when we were four years old, and our dad didn't have any yard tools. So my partner in crime and I thought it would be a great idea to go around the neighborhood and gather up all the yard tools we could find for our dad. Well, when Dad got home from work that night, he was in for a shock because there was a pile of yard tools waiting for him! We had managed to take almost all the yard tools on the block and pile them up in the back yard. When our dad saw this, he broke out in such laughter, and he called our mom out to see what we had done. We thought we were in big trouble, but Dad and Mom just laughed and thought it was so cute of us twins to do that for our dad so he could fix up the yard. Anyway, we had to return all the yard tools to the neighbors, and everyone got a good laugh out of it … except the old grump who lived at the end of street! He didn't like us twins much because we used to untie his dog all the time and let it run loose so we could play with it.

We are now forty-eight years old, and the connection we share just gets stronger over time. It's mind-boggling at times. We both sense each other's pain, our daily habits are the same, and we use a lot of the same products. There are so many stories I could share about being an identical twin, but there is not enough room here. All I can say is that it has been and will continue to be a wonderful experience—this special bond that only we as twins share.

◆   ◆   ◆

I *Don't* Like Being a Twin Because ...

People refer to us as "the twins" instead of using our names.

◆   ◆   ◆

Synchronized Singing

Melissa
Shaw AFB, South Carolina

I am a member of the U.S. Air Force and have been separated from my fraternal twin sister for the first time in my life. However, we were not always as close as we are now.

My sister has always had the strongest personality. I was often a little quiet but silently strong, so we would clash a lot in our younger years. I recall a time when we were in a store with our mother. My sister and I were in two different aisles looking at different things. I started thinking about a song from the musical *Grease,* and began to sing a verse in the middle of the song out loud. Suddenly, I heard an echo of the same verse being sung on the other side of the aisle!

I ran around the corner, hardly daring to believe this was happening, but sure enough I met my sister at the end of the aisle with a look of utter astonishment on her face that I am sure reflected mine. A few feet away, my mother was standing there looking just as disbelieving. What are the odds that two people who aren't even looking at each other or talking with each other singing a random song starting at the same random verse?

This twin connection thing is very cool, and I'm happy to say that my sister and I have grown incredibly close since then. Every reunion with her and my parents is never taken for granted.

◆   ◆   ◆

I Like Being a Twin Because ...

We have a bond that no one could ever break.

◆   ◆   ◆

Twins Miss Same Words on Spelling Test
Lisa
Huntington Beach, California

I am the mother of identical eight-year-old twin girls. They are in the second grade and in different classrooms. They both came home from school on Monday, and as we were going through one of their homework folders, I saw that one of them had taken a spelling pre-test and missed three of her words. So I pulled out her sister's spelling pre-test and was surprised to see she had missed the exact same three words! Things like this happen all the time with them.

◆   ◆   ◆

Twins Get Same Hairstyle at Different Salons
Monica Mendoza
Colorado City, Texas

My sisters are twins, and they attend school in different cities. The other day we were having a birthday party for my brother, and they arrived at separate times with the same hairstyle and identical sweaters! They were both unaware of what the other twin was going to wear. They laughed and said it never fails.

I also remember one time when they were about fifteen years old. They wanted to look different from each other, so they went to separate hair salons to get new hairstyles. When they arrived home, they found they had both chosen the exact same hairstyle!

◆   ◆   ◆

Twins Buy Each Other the Same Sweaters!
Diane Galloway
Carlsbad, California

I am an identical twin, and we are now fifty years young. I was vacationing in Colorado at my children's house over the Thanksgiving holiday while my twin stayed home in California. (We now live together again.)

I had gone to Wal-Mart the day before I was to leave, and I saw these sweaters and thought they were perfect for us. So I got my twin sister a beige sweater with speckles, and I got myself a bluish-purple speckled sweater.

The next day when I arrived at the airport, I was wearing my sweater. As I drew closer to my twin sister, I noticed that she had on the exact sweater that I had bought her! Both of us stood there with our mouths wide open and said, "I bought you a sweater just like that one!"

My twin sister had done the exact same thing while I was gone. So now we both have two sweaters.

◆   ◆   ◆

Twin Gives Same Excuse for Ear-Pulling
Simi
Dubai, United Arab Emirates

I am Simi, and my twin sister is Nimi. We both look very identical. The bond we have together is incredible. When I think about something and am about to say it, Nimi will already be saying it. When we look at anyone, we both notice the same thing. We have taken the same classes of study, got the same marks, and were first in our class. If I am incomplete in something, she will complete it. People sometimes ask whether our souls got interchanged.

Once when we were small, Nimi pulled another girl's ear, and the girl started crying. The teacher started shouting at me, and when she asked me about the situation, I knew that Nimi must have done something so I answered whatever came into my mind. I didn't even know the circumstances, but when I told Nimi about the incident later, she said, "I was about to give the same excuse!" I was thunderstruck.

One time I was in my room doing my work, and Nimi was in another room. I suddenly felt very uneasy and exhausted. I couldn't understand what was happening. Then I thought of telling Nimi about it. When I went to her, she was sitting there in silence. I asked her what was wrong, and she said she just got a spanking from our parents. Then I realized what I had felt within me!

I have always thought it's good to have a twin. I can assure you of one thing: your twin is the most understanding person in this world! You don't even have to tell your twin why you are sad because she will understand it by herself. It's always wonderful the way people stare at us and ask, "Are you Nimi or Simi?" Moreover, our birthday is on Children's Day. How wonderful!

◆   ◆   ◆

Twins Finish Each Other's Sentences
Clinton Swalley
Dunnigan, California

I have twin eight-year-old grandchildren who seem to be as normal as any other children their age. However, my story is about twin girls I met who were neighbors. They had a strange twin language where each spoke half a sentence. Twin A always started the sentence, and Twin B always finished the last half of the sentence.

Growing up, this did not present a big problem because they were always together. Then they each got married and lived apart with their husbands. Twin A had a minor problem as she had to learn to continue speaking and finish her sentences. Twin B had a major problem. She could not talk because she couldn't start sentences. It took many months to get over the hurdles.

◆   ◆   ◆

Double Trouble at Only Fifteen Months
Lisa West
Collingwood, Ontario, Canada

It has been one exciting experience raising my twin girls, Emma and Hannah. From the moment of their birth fifteen months ago, they have had an uncanny bond.

As newborns, they would only sleep when the other one was sleeping. If one would cry, the other one would start to cry. As the months went on, they became aware of each other more and more every day. If one was down for a nap and the other one was up, then the one who was awake would try to wake the sleeping twin.

Other times, they would play so intently with each other that they seemed to forget everyone else around them. As soon as one of the twins would spot her sister, she would get so excited that it was like they had not seen each other for a very long time. If one was causing mischief, she would try to get her sister in on the action.

Despite their similarities, I find both of them very strong in character in their own way. Sometimes I find that the firstborn twin, Emma, relies more on her younger twin, Hannah, to show her the way or to lead in certain things. Emma is easygoing, while Hannah is more serious. Hannah is the thinker, while Emma is more impulsive. Emma is more musically inclined than Hannah, but Hannah is more sensitive to her sister when she is upset.

Each day I wonder what they will do or encounter with each other. I am sure the next eighteen years will be one adventure after another!

◆   ◆   ◆

I Like Being a Twin Because …

I have a partner in crime.

◆   ◆   ◆

The Candy Thief
Kathy Dolan Caracciola
Bayside, New York

My sons, Ryan and Nicholas, are seven-year-old identical twins. Several days ago, just after Halloween, Ryan took a piece of candy out of Nicholas' goodie bag. As you can imagine, Nicholas was very upset and reported the incident immediately to me. After I told Ryan that he should never do that again, Ryan came up with an idea to help quell Nicholas' fears that more of his candy would be taken. He told Nicholas, "If I take any more of your candy, Mommy can punish me for a month, okay?"

Nicholas replied, "Nope, there's no way I am EVER gonna shake hands on that, Ryan. Nope, NO WAY!!! You're BOUND to do something else that's 'bold,' Mom will punish you, and then I won't have anyone to play with!"

Twins Run in the Family

The "twin connection" seems to run very strongly in certain families, with twins showing up all over the family tree! There are twins having twins, two sets of twins born to the same parents, cousins having twins, and third-generation twins! So why haven't scientists discovered that elusive "twins gene" yet?

Woman Has Twin Sons—and Twin Grandsons!

Marilyn Boren
Paris, Texas

I am the mother of twenty-six-year-old identical twin sons. I had a daughter born fifteen months after the twins arrived. (Yes, I was very busy!)

About two years ago, my daughter, now married, came out to visit and was complaining about heartburn and indigestion, and being constantly tired and moody. I told her that was easy to explain because she was pregnant with twins! My daughter was shocked because she didn't even realize that she was pregnant. She called me the next morning and told me the pregnancy test was positive! I told her I knew that, and that there were at least two in there, maybe three!

She went for her first exam with the doctor, and he confirmed her pregnancy. He sent her for an ultrasound and, sure enough, there were two little babies in there! They tried to tell her that the babies were fraternal, but I told her the babies are identical twin boys and advised her not to buy anything pink. She didn't believe me.

Finally, after a few more weeks, the sonogram revealed that she was definitely going to have twin boys. The little boys were born one week after my birthday, so I certainly consider them to be special gifts in my life. What a unique blessing to be a mother to twin sons and a grandmother to twin grandsons!

◆   ◆   ◆

A Twin Having Twins

Sherry Harrell
Clayton, Louisiana

My name is Sherry Kaye Sharp Harrell, and I have a fraternal twin whose name is Shanda Faye Sharp Roberson. We are thirty years old as I write this and are very close. We live about thirty minutes from each other, which is the farthest distance we have ever been apart. We shared the same bed (my parents had five children in five years and not enough bedrooms!) until I got married when I was eighteen years old.

Shanda is an R.N. and teaches nursing students at a university. We both graduated from college the same year, and I became a respiratory therapist. We never got the pleasure of working with each other until last year when she did some part-time work at the hospital where I worked. It was nice!

Shanda has decided to stop after having three beautiful children (one girl and two boys). I had my oldest daughter, Taylor, in 1995 (one day after our birthday on February 8), and Shanda gave birth to her beautiful little girl, Peyton, five years later on the same day!

I am due to have a cesarean section with my last pregnancy on March 24, 2006, resulting in the birth of twin boys named Titus and Timothy. Yes, I am a twin having twins! Before I knew I was expecting twins, I can remember confiding in my twin sister (we still tell each other everything) that this pregnancy was definitely different. I seemed a lot sicker than with the others, and I couldn't sleep at all the first three months.

She jokingly said, "It's because you have double the hormones carrying those twins!" I just laughed it off, but I had to make a personal trip to deliver the news to her where she was working at a hospital in the intensive care unit. She couldn't imagine what could be wrong when I showed up, standing there and glaring while I waited for her to get a moment to come out and see me.

When we finally came face-to-face, I said jokingly as I held up the sonogram pictures, "You did it to me!" Needless to say, she shared my excitement when she found out it was twins.

I am one of the few people who will be able to say that I have experienced the life of a twin full circle. I have been able to enjoy the closeness of a twin relationship with my sister. (Shanda's husband, Steve, says, "Shanda, it's your umbilical!" when I call.) And we have overcome the obstacle of constantly being compared to each other still to this day (which has never come between us). Now I get the blessing of a twin pregnancy and to see what it will be like to raise twins.

Shanda is going to be with me when I have the cesarean section because my wonderful husband, Chris, said it was just too much for him to bear when he was with me for the C-section delivery of our son, Levi. (Some people are not as interested in seeing your belly cut open as others!) Shanda is very excited to be able to experience this with me. I look forward to giving birth to twins and, Lord willing, raising and enjoying them.

I have three other children, but I have enjoyed being able to ask my own mother about issues arising from my twin pregnancy, as well as upcoming events, such as breastfeeding twins. I'm sure I will call on her often throughout the years.

The opportunity to be a twin is only half the fun for me now. When I think about raising twins, I feel truly blessed.

◆   ◆   ◆

I Like Being a Twin Because ...

We can talk about anything with each other, and we think the same.

◆   ◆   ◆

Twins Have Twins in This Family!
Stephanie
Charleston AFB, South Carolina

I don't know how doctors can say twins aren't hereditary. We have at least two sets in every generation on both sides of our family.

On my mom's side: Grandma has twin brothers, George and Benjamin (died at birth). Uncle George had twin girls, Bridget and Brenda. Grandma had twin boys, Eddie and Ellis. Mom had us, twin girls, Stephanie and Vanessa.

On my dad's side: Grandpa's brother has two sets of twins, identical boys, Kenneth and Kellis, and fraternal boy/girl twins, Paul and Carlotta. Uncle Kenneth has twin boys, Carlos and Juan. Grandpa has twin boys, Jesse and John. Dad has us.

In our family, it's scary because our twins have twins (once again, on both sides). I hope it's my sister, not me!

◆   ◆   ◆

A House Full of Twins
Dawna Kinikini
Salt Lake City, Utah

I had a single birth when I was twenty. When Hayle had just turned two, I gave birth to identical twin boys (natural). Three years later, I gave birth to twin girls (also natural). That was five kids, aged five and under!

Hayle is just turning nine now. The boys, Elias and Isaiah, are going to turn seven, and the girls, Rachel and Rebekah, are almost four. All of the kids were great as babies and are now a lot harder. The girls, however, have been a lot easier than the boys.

I love all my kids very much. My husband, Kenyon, has been in school since before we were married and is now in law school. He has one more year left, and I can't wait until he's finished. He also works twelve-hour shifts at a sleep center doing sleep studies. I stay home and take care of the kids and the house. I have a cosmetology license and sometimes I cut hair at home, but I love staying home with my kids.

◆   ◆   ◆

I *Don't* Like Being a Twin Because ...

People ask annoying questions, like if we're identical. (We're a boy and a girl!)

◆   ◆   ◆

This Family Is Overflowing with Twins
Tracey
Birkenhead, England

My mother's sister gave birth to a set of twins (a boy and a girl), and then the girl twin gave birth to a set of identical twin girls. My mother's other sister was pregnant with twins, but one didn't grow so it didn't make it. My mother had her children with no sign of twins, but to our amazement, my mother's three grandchildren also gave birth to a set of twins each! Only one set of identical twins are boys. The other two sets are boy/girl twins.

When we tell the doctors about our family, they tell us this is not hereditary. We say, "What a load of rubbish!" How can one family have so many twins and not be hereditary? Our eldest twins are forty-nine years old and the youngest are two years old.

◆   ◆   ◆

Famous Fathers of Twins

Muhammad Ali	Ivan Lendl
Ed Asner	Dave Matthews
Corbin Bernsen	Ricky Nelson
President George W. Bush	Tom Purtzer
Justin Chambers	Kenny Rogers
Sean "Diddy" Combs	Ray Romano
Elvis Costello	Dougray Scott
Patrick Dempsey	James Stewart
Robert DeNiro	Donald Sutherland
Jim Dent	Gary Trudeau
Michael J. Fox	Esera Tuaolo
Mel Gibson	Denzel Washington
Bruce Hornsby	Denis Watson
Ron Howard	Bob Woodruff

◆   ◆   ◆

Sister of Identical Twins Is Pregnant with Twins Herself
Lori Anne Mardis
Pea Ridge, Arkansas

I am the oldest sister of identical twin girls who are two and a half years younger than me. I have an eight-year-old daughter.

I found out that I was pregnant in August 2006, and I'm due on May 2, 2007. In October, I had my first ultrasound, and to our surprise we discovered I was having TWINS!

Preliminary guesses are that they, too, will be identical. To make things even more odd, I am pretty much on the same track as my mother was. She was due with my sisters on April 30th, while I am due on May 2nd.

I have my twenty-week ultrasound this Thursday and can hardly wait to see what I am having! My daddy says girls, but I think boys … we'll see!

◆   ◆   ◆

I *Don't* Like Being a Twin Because …

People get our names wrong.

◆   ◆   ◆

Twin Sisters Both Have Twins
Kim Rosu
Columbus, Ohio

My name is Kim Rosu, and I have an identical twin sister named Deena Dematteo. We have a brother who is exactly four years younger than we are. We all live within ten minutes of each other, including our parents.

We have always had a strong bond as a family, but my sister and I have a bond that only a twin would understand. She has been married to her husband Rocky for nine years, and together with him for sixteen years. They have a daughter named Marianna who is eight years old, and fraternal twins who are four years old. Their names are Laney and Kiera.

I have been married to my husband Adrian for almost five years, and we have a little girl named Tristin, who turned three in December. She is very close to her twin cousins. They see each other practically every day. They refer to each other as sisters, rather than cousins. In fact, my daughter gets mistaken for being twins with Kiera rather than the one who is actually her twin sister.

I work full-time as a department head of one of the biggest and nicest hotels in Columbus. I hired my sister part-time about a year ago. We take turns watching each other's girls while the other is at work. We had a pretty good routine down, until recently.

My husband and I had been trying to have another baby, but were not very successful. We decided to put it on hold for awhile, but once we stopped trying, I realized something wasn't right. I had been extremely sick and not feeling well. I went in for an ultrasound and was told that I was about seven weeks pregnant … and that I am having twins, too!

For now, it looks as though they may be fraternal as well, but we won't know for sure until they are born. My daughter will be four years older than her twin sisters or brothers, just like her cousin Marianna is four years older than her twin sisters. My sister and I are four years older than our brother. Oh, and Deena and I are the first set of twins in our family on both sides. I guess we just started a whole new trend!

◆   ◆   ◆

I Like Being a Twin Because …

I have someone to be with when I'm grounded, and I never get bored.

◆   ◆   ◆

Third-Generation Twins Experience Twin ESP
Rhonda

My twin sister and I are third-generation twins. Our father has a twin sister, and our maternal grandmother is an identical twin. When my own twins (boy/girl) were born, my sister was in the waiting room while I was in the operating room. When I was taken back to my room and my sister and mom joined me, my sister asked me what time the twins were born. When I told her the times, she and my mom shot each other a "look." Then my mom told me that at the moment the first baby was born, my sister had grabbed a stranger's arm in the waiting room and announced that her sister had just had a baby. Apparently, twin ESP really exists because there is no way she could have known this from where she was!

◆   ◆   ◆

Despite Family Heritage, Twins Still a Surprise!
Angela Souza
Hayward, California

I am the mother of ten-week-old fraternal twin boys. Their names are Ricky Dominic and Angel Isaac. We were definitely surprised to have twins! When we found out, we just couldn't believe it. We both have twins in our families, but we still never thought it could happen to us. The twins are also joined by their big brother, Eddy, who is going to be six years old.

So far, everything is going well. They are good babies and very healthy. They were born at thirty-six weeks, and have both already doubled their birth weight! I am so excited for this journey. I know it will be great fun!

◆   ◆   ◆

Twins Both Have Twin Pregnancies
Tina Burkhart
Stamford, Texas

My fraternal twin and I are thirty years old, and we have always shared a bond that is unbreakable. Growing up, we knew when each one was sad, sick, or happy. I remember throwing up when my sister said her stomach hurt. If we did not share the same room, we could be heard talking to each other and answering the other in our sleep. But there was no way we could have heard each other.

We had our first children, single births and boys, only eight days apart. My twin, Christi, had boy/girl twins four years ago. I felt her labor pains when she was giving birth. When I was pregnant, she told me my water was breaking before it hit the floor.

I was pregnant with identical twins that would be three years old now, but I lost them due to a violent act by an ex when I was about four months along. We also have identical twin cousins.

Being a twin creates a bond that can never be broken ... no matter the distance. Even today, I can feel my sister's emotions.

Twin Predictions

Twins don't only share psychic vibes with each other; they seem to put off some sort of sign that alerts others to their coming. Many a mom-to-be of twins has been told that she'll have twins before she has that first sonogram or even knows she's pregnant! There's something about twins ... people just KNOW!

A Guardian Angel with a Twin Premonition
Martina Goodman
San Francisco, California

Last year, my fiancé Maurice and I were on vacation in New York for New Year's Eve. We had a blast, only to find ourselves trapped in the airport a few days later when we were on our way home to San Francisco. During our fun adventure of trying to find a flight out, we met a woman who decided to start a conversation with us.

We talked about all sorts of things, including our occupations. She told us that she was a massage therapist with psychic abilities. I thought, "Yeah, right." She began to look at us like she was giving us an examination. She asked to rub my fiancé under his arm, and she told him some things about his childhood and how he still has issues around a death that happened when he was younger. I thought she was just having luck.

She continued to tell us things about Maurice's health that we had just found out. I thought again, "Lucky guess." She then asked if she could rub my shoulders. I said, "Why not?"

She began to rub my shoulders and got this weird look on her face. She said, "Do twins run in your family?" I laughed and said no, that we were not planning on having any more children. She smiled and said, "Okay, if you say so."

I thought she was crazy. She gave us her business card, and by the end of the day we had parted ways on different flights. When we reached home, we put her out of our minds.

Weeks later, I began to feel really tired and moody. I made an appointment with the doctor to see what was wrong. The nurse decided to give me a pregnancy test. It was positive! I was in shock since I was in the process of getting an IUD replacement. I didn't know what to do or say.

I went back two weeks later for an ultrasound to make sure I was pregnant and that it wasn't a mistake. The nurse began the ultrasound and got a funny look on her face. She said, "Honey, not only are you pregnant, but it's twins!"

I was at a complete loss for words until I called Maurice. He asked what happened and all I could say was, "Remember that lady in the airport?" He said yes, and I said, "We should have asked her the lottery numbers because we're having twins!"

Six weeks early, on August 24, 2006 at 10:08 and 10:10 AM, Malcolm J. Xavier and Justice J. Malik were born.

I tried to contact the psychic lady to say thank you and to let her know that she was right. But when I called her place of business, they said no one by her name had ever worked for them. Maurice and I think that maybe she was a guardian angel letting us know that our family wasn't complete yet. Whoever she was or is, she helped make our twin pregnancy a very unique one!

◆   ◆   ◆

Famous Male Twins

Mario and Aldo Andretti	Ashton Kutcher
Jose and Ozzie Canseco	Joel and Benji Madden
Aaron Carter	Gunnar and Matthew Nelson
Bucky and Rocky Covington	Elvis Presley
Vin Diesel	Dylan and Cole Sprouse
John A. Elway	Kiefer Sutherland
Robin and Maurice Gibb	Sawyer and Sullivan Sweeten
Horace Grant	Justin Timberlake
Paul and Morgan Hamm	Billy Dee Williams

◆   ◆   ◆

Girl Predicts Twin Sisters Will Be Born
Shianne Moales
Bridgeport, Connecticut

I am twenty-one years old and the mother of a beautiful three-year-old. When I found out I was pregnant for a second time, I was not ready to be a mother again, so I was contemplating an abortion. But a voice inside of me kept preventing me from making it to my appointments. Finally, I decided to keep the pregnancy.

As my first ultrasound neared, I would ask my daughter if she wanted a brother or a sister. She would continuously respond, "Mommy, I am going to have two sisters." I would just laugh her off as a joke. Finally, the day came for the ultrasound, and lo and behold there were two baby girls floating around in there. They say the kids always know!

I am now twenty-seven weeks pregnant with identical twin girls, and I am very excited. I will be happier when I can welcome my baby girls into this world!

◆   ◆   ◆

I *Don't* Like Being a Twin Because …

We have to share everything.

◆   ◆   ◆

Older Brother's Dream Predicts Twins
Jo Kovaleski
Dallas Center, Iowa

My twins were actually dreamt about by their older brother when I wasn't even pregnant with them yet. It was freaky to become pregnant three months later with the very boys he had dreamed about! My twins aren't identical, but they are very connected. When one is in pain or upset, the other seems to have a bad day or get sick as well. They are in separate classrooms now, but this still happens!

◆   ◆   ◆

I Like Being a Twin Because …

We are never lonely.

◆   ◆   ◆

Dead Granddad Sends Twin Daughters
Chantelle Rennicks
Nottingham, England

I was told from a very early age that I could never have children due to an accident I had when I was two years old. So as I grew up with this knowledge, took classes at school in childcare, and did loads of babysitting for friends and family, I learned to accept the fact that I would never become a mum. Nonetheless, it made me love children and everything about them. I'd look at all my friends and envy them because they had something I was always told I couldn't have. Then, in 2004, I lost my granddad just two weeks before my twentieth birthday. I was really close to him, and I took it very hard when he passed away.

Three months later, I went to see a clairvoyant, and she told me that within eighteen months I would become pregnant and have my dream of being a mum because my granddad had made it happen. I found this hard to believe because of the accident, but on the other hand my granddad knew this had always been my only dream.

Time went on, and I didn't think anything more of it. I started dating a guy. He knew about me not being able to have children, and he was fine with that because he didn't want any. In the end, everything didn't go as planned and we went our separate ways—only for me to find out four weeks later that I was eight weeks pregnant!

I didn't believe it was real at first. It took a while to sink in. It was only when I went for my very first scan that I believed it—and that's when I found out I was having twins! I was over the moon, but the father was not. I had my twins at thirty-nine weeks exactly. Now five weeks later, I have two beautiful baby girls whom I wouldn't change for the world.

I thank my granddad every day for this gift. I know he will always watch over and protect them. And I will do my best to give them the best life I can and make my granddad proud. I know he looks down at me every day with a smile on his face, knowing he has made me the happiest I've ever been in my life because I have something precious twice over—the love of my special girls.

◆   ◆   ◆

I *Don't* Like Being a Twin Because …

When you get angry at your twin, they're always there. You can't escape!

◆   ◆   ◆

Trick Turns into Real Twins
Sue Hantz
Turlock, California

I'm the grandmother of ten-year-old twin boys, Brandon and Bradley. This story is from before they were born. Actually, it is from before the brother before them was born. He is eighteen days short of being a year older than the twins.

My daughter (their mother) was working at a hospital, and at the time they were promoting ultrasounds. They asked her if she wanted to do one, which she did, and somehow they took the image of the one baby and flipped it upside down to make it appear as if there were two babies!

So, she took it home and showed her husband. Just about the time he started to calm down, she told him it was a joke. We all thought that was so funny!

Well, that baby was born a single, but a couple of months later, they were over at my house and my son-in-law said, "I think we are pregnant again."

My daughter was sent to get an ultrasound to see how far along she was, and she was told she was having twins! She began to cry. When she got back to my house, I could tell something was wrong. I asked her about it, and she started to cry again. She said she was having twins. I reassured her it was okay, and she said her husband wasn't ever going to believe her after the trick she had played on him from the last baby!

◆   ◆   ◆

I Like Being a Twin Because …

We always finish each other's sentences.

◆   ◆   ◆

Woman Believes She Is a "Twinless Twin"
Carol

I believe I have a twin sister, even though I have no documentation at this time. All I have is a feeling that I can't explain. At times it's very strong and comes from deep inside. I can tell you there's something missing.

I tried to find out why, but my mother would only say, "Get out of my past." I did not understand since my questions had nothing to do with her. Three years ago, I said to another family member, "I have a feeling something is missing in my life." Her reply was, "Yes, I understand, Carol, and I have a document to prove it."

I believe I am a twinless twin separated at birth.

Being a Twin Is a Blessing

Most twins will tell you they love being a twin! They know each other better than anyone else ever can. And their families feel the same way. Parents know they're very blessed to have twins. It's a very special experience for the entire family!

Together for Life
Michele Christian
Braintree, Massachusetts

I remember it like it was yesterday: the nurse revealing the results of my in-vitro pre-transfer. "You have two grade A embryos. Now, remember, you did so well the first time that you may only want to put back one of those embryos. However, even if you put two back, chances are it would probably only result in one baby." I simply told her no, we would transfer two embryos, and God would take it from there. So, two embryos were transferred and, you guessed it, the result was TWINS! Two beautiful girls, Emily and Sara. I often wonder, *What if I had chosen to transfer only one embryo? Which one would not be here today? Emily or Sara?* Imagine what I would have taken away from one of these perfect girls—their best friend, their soul mate for life!

Emily and Sara are almost six years old now, and since their birth they have had an incredible bond. Immediately after they were born, they were swaddled together in their crib, sucking each other's fingers and breathing softly on each other's faces. It is tough for them to be separated at any time. One cold Christmas Eve, when the girls were two years old, they both came down with a terrible flu, and I had to take them to the ER. As Sara was being weighed, Emily had to remain in triage. Being so sick, they couldn't bear to be apart, so they were both screaming for each other. Emily would wail, "Where's Yaaa Yaaa?!" (That was how she said "Sara" at the time.) Sara could hear her crying and would yell back, "AIEEEEE!" (Emily). It was so heartbreaking to listen to them. When they were brought back together, they just stared at each other with tear-filled eyes as if to say, "Thank God, you're here!"

When they were teething, they would each get the same teeth on the same exact day! I found it strange since Emily and Sara are fraternal twins with completely different body types. Coincidence happens once or twice. But every time? There is no explanation! They finish each other's sentences and thoughts. At times, they have a communication that only they can understand. One will start a funny story about an experience they shared, the other will naturally pick up midstream to finish it, and they will both end up laughing hysterically. They are my Thelma and Louise.

I never had a sister to share experiences with, so I can live vicariously through my twins' relationship. To this day, they still sleep together. I'm not sure why I bothered to have two beds. They shared a crib, then Emily's bed, and lately they sleep on the floor because it's like camping. They use a body pillow instead of a standard one so they can share it. In the middle of the night, if one gets up and tries to come in with me, the other one is sure to follow. Being without each other is not an option.

They were in the same class at preschool last year, and there was an incident where Emily was not invited into the "girls club" their friends had created. I suppose it was a simple oversight on the part of the other female classmates to omit Emily, but she came home completely devastated. Sara went to school the next day and demanded that Emily be in the club or she was out. I was so proud to see that they will stand up for one another.

This year, however, they are starting kindergarten and will not be in the same class. I have decided it is time to separate them so they may seek out their own individuality. I know as they get older, they will protect each other, and probably hide secrets from me and cover for the other. They will get their driver's licenses together, go to the prom together, and graduate high school together. And that's just the beginning! They have so many experiences to share. Disbelief runs through me as I try to imagine what life would be like for the other if one were not here. It's just inconceivable. I'm sure they would have their friends, toys, and interests, and would not know any different. But what they have now with each other is priceless, treasured and unique. They each share a part of their soul with each other. They have that one person (other than their parents) who will say, "I am always here for you."

As parents, we only spend the first half of our children's lives with them. We are not there to guide them through middle age and retirement. Of course, Emily and Sara will have their brother and friends with them as the years go by. But these two will have each other for life. Each of us goes through life alone, but with twins it is different. They are molded together: same blood, same feelings, loving each other unconditionally for life. The bond is powerful and phenomenal.

◆   ◆   ◆

Girls Talk to Each Other in Their Sleep
Patty Roland
Grinnell, Iowa

I am the exceptionally blessed adoptive mother of what I presume to be identical twin girls, seven years old. I say "presume" because I have no official documentation that they are identical, only the fact that I, on most days, get them confused! They are also very close. They won't sleep apart. They say (and I have no reason to doubt) that they can feel one another's pain, and they have many of the other typical twin characteristics.

A couple of nights ago, I checked on the girls before I went to bed. Although they were spooning (typical for them), they had kicked off their blanket. I was attempting to re-cover them without waking them, but one of the girls stirred, acted as though she was awake, scooted to the side of the bed (as if she were looking for something under the bed), and started talking in her sleep. Her sister was completely out at this point, but as soon as the one stopped talking, the other sat straight up in bed and appeared to be answering her, after which she very promptly laid her head right back down.

Can twins be so close that they can actually participate in one another's dreams?! Was it just a coincidence, or am I plain crazy? My girls truly amaze me every day in every way, and I am very blessed to have them.

◆   ◆   ◆

Telepathic Twins
Aiya Bryan
Silver City, New Mexico

I am a mother of identical twin boys, Gabriel and Ethan. When they were four, my mother wanted to spend some time with them, but she was never able to handle both of them at the same time. We decided to let Gabriel go for a visit for three days, and then Ethan would go for three days.

Ethan and I were driving in the car on our way to make the switch. He was sitting in his car seat as quiet as can be, just looking out the window, when he told me, "Mom, tell Gabriel to get his clothes on." I looked at him and told him that Gabriel was with Grandma, but he said, "Just tell him, Mom. He needs to get his clothes on."

So I called my mom out of curiosity and asked if she was having a hard time getting Gabriel dressed. She said yes, they were having an argument because Gabriel didn't want to get dressed as it was too cold and he wanted to stay in his jammies!

I was so amazed. You hear about these stories where twins are so connected even when they are miles and miles apart, but when you witness it for yourself it is just mind-blowing. I am sure I will have more stories to tell as they get older. It just makes me realize how blessed I am to be a mother of twins.

◆   ◆   ◆

Many Reasons to Love Being a Twin
Emily Fields
United Kingdom

Being a twin can sometimes have its downsides, but there are more reasons for good than there are for bad. For example:

1. We always have someone to talk to.

2. Someone is always there for us.

3. Someone truly understands us.

4. If you're identical (like my twin and I), you can always freak people out by speaking at the same time, walking in step, etc.

5. We always have someone to play with.

These are just some of the reasons I like being a twin. But overall, the number-one reason why I love being a twin is because we are different … we have something that many people would love to be. I wouldn't give up being a twin for the world!

◆   ◆   ◆

I *Don't* Like Being a Twin Because …

She's older by ten minutes, but she still thinks that makes her superior!

◆   ◆   ◆

No Bond Like It in the World
Rita Howard
Chickamauga, Georgia

My name is Rita, and I have an identical twin, Anita. She is the oldest by six minutes. Our mother didn't even know she was having twins until we were born!

We love being twins. However, as children we hated being "the twins" and having to share everything. About the time we were in third grade, we stopped dressing alike, and Anita cut her hair short.

We didn't begin dressing alike and having the same haircut again until we were about twenty-five years old and began going to twin gatherings such as the Twins Days and the International Twins Association yearly convention.

We have so many "coincidences" in our lives. When we married, both of our last names had the same beginning letter (Hayes and Howard). Both of our husbands had March birthdays and were physically similar. Their names were also similar in their structures, beginning with two consonants, a vowel, and ending with double t (Wyatt and Scott). We divorced within months of each other because we just couldn't stand our husbands coming between us!

We both have two boys. Three of our boys have similar names. Her oldest is William Rhett (he's called Rhett); her youngest is Liam (which is the Irish form of William). My youngest is William (he's called Will), and if you combine Will and Liam, you get … William. We did not plan this. In fact, we didn't even notice it until some time after Will was born. Another coincidence with our oldest boys is that they were both born on the tenth of the month (different months). There are so many more coincidences, but it would take forever to list them all!

Growing up, we never noticed that we were mirror-image twins. Just a couple of years ago, Anita asked me one day, "Do you always carry your purse on your left shoulder?" She always carries her on the right. Since we noticed that, I began parting my hair on the opposite side so we can "look in the mirror" when we see each other.

We're usually on the same side of all our pictures together. There are only a few where we switched sides. We do have very different careers. She is an insurance agent, and I am a teacher. We live approximately 100 miles apart, so it's always a treat to have her come to my class and trick my students and coworkers. We've also tricked her coworkers, and they never knew until we told them! We've confused our parents, too. Most people tell us apart by the children we have with us. But our mother has at times thought I was Anita with Rita's kids, and vice versa!

Anita's youngest son has always had a difficult time telling who was his mom. Even as a small baby, he'd cry relentlessly when I'd leave because he thought his mom was leaving him. He's almost eight years old now and has to look at our name necklaces to tell us apart.

We have such a close bond that it amazes and even baffles some people. We always know what the other one is thinking. We've had people comment about how we move in unison when we're together, and that we seem like a whole person when we're together. And that's exactly how we feel when we're together.

There is no bond like it in the world.

◆   ◆   ◆

I Like Being a Twin Because …

We can play pranks, and being a twin makes our lives more interesting.

◆   ◆   ◆

Grandmother's Spirit Comes to the Rescue
Stephanie Sylvain
Mansfield, Massachusetts

Twenty-eight weeks … it was supposed to be a routine doctor's visit and ultra-sound. It turned out to be anything but.

I was feeling great and was in absolute disbelief when the doctor told me I was in labor and needed to head over to labor and delivery to be monitored. There had to be a mistake. I couldn't be in labor because I felt fine. But indeed I was, and the day passed in a blur of medication to stop my contractions, along with visits from various doctors.

Someone came by from the NICU and told me all the medical issues that twenty-eight-week-old babies could have. I signed a consent form for a C-section and many other papers. I pretty much signed whatever was put in front of me if I thought it could make this nightmare stop.

But it wasn't stopping, and by the evening, I was four centimeters dilated. The doctor told me that she would be back in an hour, and if I was still progressing, we would start discussing the plan for the twins' birth. It was at that moment of my medication-induced haze that I really fell apart. I couldn't believe this was happening. It was all so sudden and so very frightening. I called to the one person who I felt could save me: my grandmother Josephine.

We had lost Josie only seven months earlier. It was a sudden loss and a tremendous one to my family. She passed away during the IVF cycle that led to the twins' conception. I had always felt that she had sent the gift of the twins to us. And so I called to her, and she heard me.

When the doctor came back an hour later, my labor had stopped. With bed rest for the duration of my pregnancy, I was able to carry my twins until thirty-six weeks. Looking back, that was the worst night of my life. The uncertainty was overwhelming. So many things could have gone differently, and life could have been forever changed. But we were blessed exactly eight weeks after that night with beautiful, healthy twins who were able to come home with us two days after their birth. I think about what could have been, and it brings me to tears.

Their birth ended up being everything I had imagined. I did not need a C-section, and I felt incredibly calm through the whole thing. I will never know how Eva, "my peanut," kept her brother, John (the larger of the two), from making an early arrival. I will forever give her the credit when telling them the story of their "near" birth. And, of course, credit needs to go to Josie. And it has, with Eva being given the middle name of Josephine.

◆　　　◆　　　◆

Twins' Children Have Same Birthday
Tanya Clark
Troy, Illinois

My twin brother and I have been extremely close since birth. Even though he is a boy and I am a girl, we have always shared the same friends and stayed very close. To this day, we talk daily, and up until a few months ago, he lived with me and my family.

We are twenty-eight years old now. I have two kids. The oldest is a girl. With my son, I was due July 2, 2002, but I went into labor with him on June 20 and delivered him the next day, on June 21.

Several months later, my brother was expecting his first son. His girlfriend was not due until June 28, but she was starting to have some complications with her pregnancy, so her doctor decided to set her induction for June 23.

But on June 20 at 7:30 in the morning, she went into labor. She went to the hospital, only to be sent back home due to irregular contractions. However, she ended up back at the hospital that night in full-blown labor. The nurse said she expected her to have the baby that night, but her labor slowed again.

She finally delivered the baby on June 21, my son's birthday. As boy and girl twins who have stayed so close, my brother and I are thrilled that his son was born on my son's birthday!

◆   ◆   ◆

I *Don't* Like Being a Twin Because ...

When she has a party, I have to come.

◆   ◆   ◆

Perhaps There Is a "Twin Thing" ...
Bronia
Derbyshire, England

I'm a fraternal twin, but my sister and I are close even though we are very different people. People have always asked us if we have a "twin thing," some sort of special connection, to which I always said no. But recently, weird things have started to happen. For instance, when she stays at other people's houses, I can't sleep, which is odd because I always fall asleep in the middle of whatever we're watching on TV! On Boxing Day, we were messing about, dancing in between the rooms in our house, and we kept doing the exact same things! So, maybe we've got a "twin thing" after all!

◆   ◆   ◆

Born to Be a Mother of Twins
Marlene Fox
Prospect, Connecticut

A friend of mine and I got pregnant around the same time. My friend had in vitro fertilization, so I joked with her that she was going to have twins. Well, she didn't, but I did!

I had never even thought it could be a possibility. The day I found out was the absolute happiest day of my life. I went for an ultrasound because of a problem I was having. It seemed to take forever, so finally I asked the ultrasound tech if she had seen a heartbeat. She said yes, that everything was fine. She then called my husband into the room, turned the monitor toward us, and said, "Here's baby A and here's baby B." I thought I was going to fall off the table. I started crying and laughing at the same time and said, "What am I going to do with two of them?"

After we got out of the appointment, naturally we wanted to show everyone the pictures of the ultrasound to see if they could figure out that we were having twins. Well, to see the looks on our families' faces and the tears of happiness in their eyes was the best thing in the world.

I had two boys on April 14, 2005, the second happiest day of my life. They're amazing and do the funniest things. I feel as though I was born to be a mother of twins. It's the best thing ever!

◆   ◆   ◆

Twin Won't Let Mother Punish His Brother
Sharon Harary
Brooklyn, New York

My twin two-year-old boys love each other so much that when one boy hurts the other one, and I try to punish the troublemaker, his brother who got hurt yells back at me to protect him! If I punish the child by giving him a time-out, the other twin always wants to be punished, too, even if he just got hurt. He just always wants to be with his brother!

◆   ◆   ◆

Miracle Twin Boys
Lilly Ewert
Littleton, Colorado

I am the mother of twenty-four-month-old identical twin boys. I had been unable for many years to have children due to a very serious heart condition. When I married at forty, I was told my heart was strong enough that I could probably carry a child, but I was also told I had only a 1 percent chance of getting pregnant.

My then husband and I tried unsuccessfully to get pregnant for over a year. We began fertility treatments, with two failed attempts. We were then scheduled for in vitro, taking two months off to start a natural fertility treatment that I had researched and put together.

We became pregnant naturally the month before we were scheduled for in vitro. At six weeks, an ultrasound determined we were having identical twins! They were born via C-section on May 31, 2004, at just over six pounds each, three weeks and one day prior to their due date. They are very healthy little boys, and are mirror-image twins—one is left-handed and the other right-handed. They are our little miracles!

◆   ◆   ◆

I Like Being a Twin Because ...

It's like carrying on a conversation with yourself without people thinking you're crazy.

◆   ◆   ◆

Twin Brother Is Sister's Protector
Karen Meyer
Reno, Nevada

My twin brother, Kevin, took verbal and physical abuse to protect me. When our mom gave us and our little brother away because of drug and alcohol abuse, Kevin always felt bad that he got to live with our grandparents, and I went to a foster home. My little brother went to live with his grandparents. My twin has always been the protector, and we still talk on the phone sometimes.

◆   ◆   ◆

Different States, Same Connection
Leanne Reese
North Vernon, Indiana

Although my twin sister, Debbie, and I are forty-one years old and have lived in different states for more than twenty years, our connection still keeps showing up in uncanny ways. For instance, I will call her on the phone, and she will be fixing the exact same dinner that I am fixing, right down to the very same time I am cooking!

One Mother's Day, we each sent our mother a card—and the cards were identical!

Other fun facts: Our husbands both have sisters with the same birthday. And our last names are also first names (Reese and Morgan).

These are just a few of the many ways in which my sister and I continue to have our "twin connection"!

◆   ◆   ◆

Twins "Get" Each Other
Lena

I love being a twin because it is my normality, my special identity, and it means there is a world that only exists between me and my sister that no one else can understand or have access to, not even our husbands.

It's reassuring to know that there is another person alive who "gets me" and whom I know intricately. We share the exact same genetic makeup, think in similar ways, speak in similar ways, and "get" each other without the need to speak.

I cannot imagine being a singleton, nor do I imagine that it can be much fun. Twins always have someone the same age as them, who speaks the same language. They discover and learn about things in their development around the same time. So we always have our equal in every sense with whom to explore and discover things.

The gap between "getting" the grown-up world is unimportant to us, whereas a single child or one with siblings of various and differing ages is always confronted by confusing clashes of the adult conversational world.

I know that my sister has always been with me since the genesis of our very existence. I'm sure we must have had some kind of awareness of each other even in our mother's womb. Perhaps we even played with each other there.

The other best thing about being a twin is knowing exactly how something would look on me by seeing what it looks like on my sister. When we were teenagers, rather than buying clothes that looked alike, we bought two sets of different looks so that we could get more for our money.

My sister is the dominant one, and I suspect that must have been the case in the womb as well. I am quite happy to be the quieter one.

◆   ◆   ◆

Twins Have the Same Feelings
Nyria Alonzo

I am twenty-eight years old, and I have a twin sister who was born a minute earlier than me. The biggest reason I love being a twin is that since I was born, I have had someone who goes through the same exact feelings. I can tell when something is wrong with my twin; I can feel her sadness even though we are miles apart.

When you have a twin, you have someone who will always be there with you, someone to share your life with.

I also love that you can get away with so many things with your parents. Everywhere we go, people are amazed because we are twins, which is cool. They all want to have a twin and ask us how it feels!

◆   ◆   ◆

God Blessed Them Twice
Stacey Stuhrenberg
Fort Dodge, Iowa

We had difficulties getting pregnant and had to use fertility treatments with all three of our children. The first one was born a singleton, and the last two were twins. It only took a couple of treatments to conceive our first child, but when we tried for our second child, we had to go through six treatments. We had discussed how long we should try the treatments before coming to the conclusion that we would be a one-child family, and had decided that procedure #6 was going to be the last time.

Well, I believe that God's plan was to test us, because a few weeks after procedure #6, we found out that we were pregnant. When we went and had the first ultrasound, it showed that we had two embryos. The doctor said that in some cases one of the embryos sometimes doesn't make it, but our little angels stayed nice and strong throughout the whole pregnancy and are now perfect little girls who just recently celebrated their first year of life here on Earth.

I guess that God blessed us twice for our patience in waiting for them!

◆   ◆   ◆

Being a Twin Is Special
Karen Meyer
Reno, Nevada

When I was little, my twin brother was always a kind and loving person. We were best friends and protected our little brother. My brother struggles when we are separated, but he always says how loving I am and doesn't believe me when I tell him he is also loving.

I love being a twin because I know there is someone who really loves me for me.

I love being a twin because it makes me feel special.

I love being a twin because when I call to wish my twin brother a special birthday, he giggles and wishes me a happy birthday, too.

◆   ◆   ◆

"Identical" Twin Brothers Were Most Likely Fraternal
Barbara
Hadley, Massachusetts

I remember vividly the cold January morning we came downstairs and found out that Mama had TWO babies in the bassinette beside her bed. A doctor who had recently returned from tending our servicemen during WWII went directly to a dance hall where he bragged that he had just delivered his first twins, and so everyone in our little town knew it before we did.

Fannie had come to take care of us and our house, and to make sure Mama spent the required ten days in bed. None of us liked her cooking and wished she wasn't there, but Mama kept having babies so fast that Daddy kept Fannie for several years.

There had been a brother, a sister, another brother and then two sisters—all separate births between me and the twins. Mama's habit was to have us "visit" our new sibling one at a time in her room. She would introduce us and let us hold the infant and tell us to talk to it for a few minutes before she allowed us to give it a kiss on the cheek.

Fannie made a big show of escorting my three older sisters in to see our twins and then announced that she wasn't going to allow me into Mama's room because I was "sick."

Mama yelled, "Who's sick?"

"Barbara."

"What's the matter with her?"

"She's got a cold. She's coughing." (I had never coughed.)

Mama said she didn't hear any coughing, and they argued about me seeing the twins until Mama got out of bed and came to the kitchen.

Fannie didn't know that when all the other children had chickenpox, measles, and whooping cough, I didn't catch anything, nor that the doctor had told Mama he thought I was naturally immune to diseases. So, Mama knew I didn't have a cold.

Once Mama determined that Fannie apparently thought she was in charge of EVERYTHING, she told Fannie she was to let me in to see the babies if she knew what was good for her. And I decided I wasn't going to mind Fannie, no matter what. I refused to move from my chair, and she soon found out she wasn't strong enough to pull me to my feet. And calling on my three older sisters didn't help. I didn't stand until Mama called to me. Then I went in her room and cried the whole time as I held one twin first, and then the other.

Only Mama knew which twin was which for about three months. She only knew because she kept a tiny gold safety pin in the sleeve of the firstborn.

At around three months, they started looking more and more different. By the time they were four months old, David's blond hair and blue eyes had turned brown, while Donald's remained. Eventually, David looked like Mama's male relatives, and Donald looked like Daddy's father.

Mama said the doctor had told her the twins were identical because there was only one placenta, and she went to her grave wondering why her identical twins didn't look like one another at all. She'd talk about it and then tell whoever was listening how much they ACTED alike.

When they grew up, they frequently sent her the same Mother's Day cards, and if one sent a few dollars, the other did also—and it would be the same amount! No matter where they lived or how much money they made, they seemed to gravitate into stores where they purchased the exact same pieces of clothing.

However, my adult twin brothers' appearances remained completely different. David was about six inches shorter than Donald and had a different body build. David had a heart attack at age thirty-two and died less than twenty years later. He married, fathered four children, and always stayed close to home.

Donald also married, fathered three sons, divorced, married a second time, and has constantly gone from woman to woman since he ended his first marriage.

My daughter is a midwife, and she told me that sometimes when space is at a premium in the womb, the two placentas of fraternal twins meld and it only looks like one when they're born. Donald weighed 7 lbs., 7 ounces, and David weighed 7 lbs., 2 ounces. Either infant outweighed the average male. I think originally there were two placentas, and they did meld due to crowding.

◆   ◆   ◆

Being a Twin Is a Gift
Daniela Cerezo Reynoso
Queretaro, Mexico

There's one question that has been asked of me for as long as I can remember: "How does it feel to be a twin?" In my heart, I always have the same answer: "Being a twin is a gift you are blessed with. It is the certainty of knowing there is one person in the world who truly understands you, fulfills you, gives you support and loves you. Being a twin could be described as having the magnificent chance of coming with your best of everything to this experience that we call life."

Mariana and I were born twenty-three years ago. We have always had what I call a pretty normal twin relationship. We could always fight between the two of us, but if someone tried to get involved or defend one of us, surely we would join forces against the intruder.

We have our code; we understand each other without words. We share the same friends. We are similar in many things, but we are opposites in many others.

We have had some unexplainable twin situations, one of which happened just a few years ago, when we were teenagers. I had a really important discussion with my father. I was so angry, sad and disappointed that I decided to leave my house. Mariana wasn't at home, as she was hanging out with some friends, but without knowing why, she started crying and had this desperate feeling to talk with me. So she called home, and when she asked for me, our mom told her what had happened. She went to the place where she knew she could find me and calmed me down. And she persuaded me to come back home with her!

We are best friends. I feel Mariana, as the older twin, protects me and is like my conscience. I have never felt this unconditional love from anybody else. I love my twin as I know I can't love anybody else.

◆   ◆   ◆

Twins Love to Share Their Lives
Deborah Kerchner
Maryland

My twins are so happy they are twins. They are almost always smiling! They love to be around each other, playing, nursing, sharing their lives. They just became one-year-olds. When one tries something new, the other comes right over and wants to do the same thing. It is a riot. They don't seem to mind when the other one climbs on him, pokes him, or grabs his hair. They even grab food from each other's trays at the same time!

They are similar, monozygotic or identical, but different. They have a few defining differences. The younger one is louder, and is heard anywhere in the house. When he is up, he wakes the other every time.

The older one is quieter and a little more patient, so waiting his turn is easier for him. He is the one who loves his brother even more. It is amazing because the smiles he gives his brother are so special. He was born eleven minutes earlier, and when his baby twin brother is not in his crib and he is put down first, he cries and wails and will not go to sleep until the other one is put down in his crib, which is next to his.

It is not the case the other way. The younger one will just settle down with his security blanket and thumb, with his tushy in the air, not noticing where his brother is. By the way, they both suck their left thumb and do the same thing with their blankets and tushies!

◆　　◆　　◆

Twin Brothers Are Alike ... Yet Different
Benjamin
Rock Springs, Georgia

My identical twin, Zach, and I were both born on October 29, 1985, only seven minutes apart. Growing up, my parents used to dress me in blue and Zach in red so they could tell us apart. To this day, even though we're now twenty-one years old, people still get us mixed up all the time. Zach and I chose the same careers, and we drive the same cars and motorcycles. Our personalities are even identical.

Even though we live 200 miles apart, we still talk on the phone every day and see each other at least once a month. We've even keep our hairstyles like the other.

When we both turned eighteen, we got our first tattoos together. It's amazing because I don't see any difference between us, but everybody says, "You two are so much alike, but yet so different." I'll never know what they mean, but it's okay.

One thing I really like about being a twin is that we are always there for each other, whether or not we agree with the other.

About Twin Connections

The Twin Connections website at www.twinconnections.com was started by Debbie LaChusa, a fraternal twin, to celebrate the unique and often mysterious bond that connects twins. If you're a twin, you've undoubtedly experienced it. If you're a parent, sibling or friend of twins, you've witnessed it. Twin Connections is a place for you to share your twin story, read twin stories, share and view twin photos, learn about famous twins and interesting twin news, and join a community of twins and twins' parents. You may also see photos of many of the twins whose stories were included in this book on the Twin Connections website.

If you have an amazing or interesting twin story of your own, you are invited to submit it for publication on the Twin Connections website, which entertains more than 10,000 visitors every month with its growing collection of twin stories and photos!

Visit www.twinconnections.com today!

978-0-595-47944-3
0-595-47944-8

Made in the USA
Columbia, SC
15 February 2021